“A leader must have the courage to act against an adjuration and admonishment advice.”

ACKNOWLEDGEMENT

Many thanks to all for their contagious drive, unsuppressed brand building and ongoing support. Many Owners of new start-ups, executives and CEOs helped me in forming management techniques for the future that will be required for the attainment of the desired goals of a particular firm. This book is the amalgamation of many management techniques and rules required to be formed for an organisation to function efficiently and effectively. These techniques meet all the requirements that need to be adopted to stay in the competitive market for the long term and work sedulously and assiduously for the attainment of the desired goal of a company.

CONTENT

INTRODUCTION

"Management is about arranging and telling. Leadership is about nurturing and enhancing."

From the working title for the book, "THE NEW TECHNIQUES REQUIREMENTS FOR MANAGEMENT", you can understand that this book contains all the important aspects of new management requirements for the firm to run smoothly and effectively for the attainment of the desired goals of a particular firm in the competitive market.

Many management books which are available in the market teach youth that management techniques are like an "old vine in a new bottle".

The ideas are the same just with a new form of words, but the real business world is completely contradictory to the theories of different books. The ideas of one particular book do not define the exact reality of the business world when one person runs a business practically in a competitive market. This book will figure out the materialistic techniques required for a firm to run in the competitive market and the tools required to fight with rival competitors in the real market.

The world market is like a battlefield where you need to take right decisions and need to make the right strategies to fight against the enemy on a battlefield. This book might help you to understand the strategies required to fight the world market competition against a rival firm. So just close your eyes and imagine and envisage this world as a battlefield and also visualise your company as a kingdom and employees as a soldier.

(Let's begin the journey of the new world)

While closing your eyes imagine fighting on the battlefield against the enemy which in reality fetch as a competitor in the business world. You know that "Imagination is your invisible power to produce all things powerful". Now imagine the techniques you would use to fight against your foe on the battlefield; the same technique but with a transformation in the process is required to fight the enemy in the world market.

"Practice Golden-Rule 1 of Management in everything you do. Manage others in business the way you would like to be managed."

Managing is not a very easy process. First and foremost, you need to come out of different kinds of illusions you form by reading a few books about the real market world. You cannot learn swimming by reading a book but a book can only help you in understanding the knowledge and techniques of the process of swimming. For swimming, you need to go into the deep water, similarly, for understanding the techniques you need to apply this management process in real-life business.

Now for understanding the management first let's talk about the leadership style, traits and qualities of Sir Bill Gates who is an American business magnate, software developer, investor, author, philanthropist and most importantly the co-founder of Microsoft.

Leadership Style Traits, Skills and Qualities

Bill Gates is an interesting study when looking at leadership styles. He is the antithesis of what one would expect from a leader. He dropped out of school, pursued a dream, and took risks based on his personal knowledge and creativity instead of what others had taught him.

Those risks paid off for Gates. He often trades spots with Jeff Bezos, one of the richest people in the world.

His leadership style is one that would be included in the descriptions of a transformational leader. That is because he followed a strong vision, had a passion for the work he was doing, and that emotion helped to energize the people who would start following him.

Key Attributes of Transformational Leadership

Bill Gates focused on transformational leadership because that style came naturally to him. He could adapt to other types of leadership when the need arose, but for the most part, his time at Microsoft was dominated by this leadership style.

The qualities of a transformational leader include the following points of emphasis.

- There is a desire to encourage personal creativity in oneself and the rest of the team.
- Support and encouragement are provided at the individual level instead of focusing this resource on team-based perspectives.
- Motivation is individualized and inspirational, with clear communication coming from the leader to promote a specific path toward an end result.

The development of trust from followers leads to respect because there is evidence provided that the ideas being implemented will actually work.

It is because of these qualities that many of the people who started working for Gates began to emulate his leadership style.

Traits of the Bill Gates Leadership Style

There are 6 clear traits that are a fundamental part of how Bill Gates approaches the concept of leadership.

1. Focus

Knowing something is much different from having wisdom. Gates focuses on the one thing he knows best, which is software, and then he makes it the best it can become. He worked hard to dominate his industry, made execution a top priority, and stuck with the skills that he considered to be his strongest. You can still see this focus through the work he does with his charitable foundation.

2. Big Picture

Gates also takes a practical approach to setting goals. He has a big picture that he keeps in mind. Instead of creating a vision that is unapproachable, Gates uses a step-based approach to make progress toward his vision. It's like trying to walk up a staircase. With this leadership style, you're taking one step at a time instead of trying to jump from the bottom to the top.

3. Creativity

Instead of staying in a zone of comfort, Gates encouraged himself and his people to embrace creativity. His leadership style works to empower people because individual perspectives create new opportunities to explore ideas. Although some people followed him because of the charisma he exudes, many people followed Gates because they knew he could help them transform themselves into better leaders too.

4. Caring

Even though Gates is often listed as one of the richest people in the world, he is also one of the most prolific givers to philanthropic causes in the world today. In 2010, Gates (with Warren Buffett) promised to give away a majority of his wealth. Over $28 billion has been donated to his foundation, with the goal of giving away $90 billion in time. That caring attitude was also present in the workplace, making sure people had the best possible opportunity to find success if they wanted it.

5. Education

Bill Gates may have dropped out of school, but that doesn't mean he ignores what a good education is able to provide. Learning is a lifelong process under his leadership style. There is always something new to learn every day if one is willing to look for it in their life. Even after he helped to found Microsoft and built it into a software empire, Gates was working on his public speaking skills, his communication skills, and ways that he could improve social interactions with others.

6. Passionate

Love Microsoft products or hate them, there is no denying the fact that Gates put a lot of love into everything he did for the company. Even if the only thing he needed to do was write a thank you note, you were guaranteed a message that came straight from his heart. Like many transformational leaders, the belief of Bill Gates is that if something is worth doing, then it is worth doing to the best of one's ability.

CHAPTER 1

MARKETING

Marketing management is the organizational discipline that focuses on the practical application of marketing orientation, techniques and methods inside enterprises and organizations and on the management of a firm's marketing resources and activities.

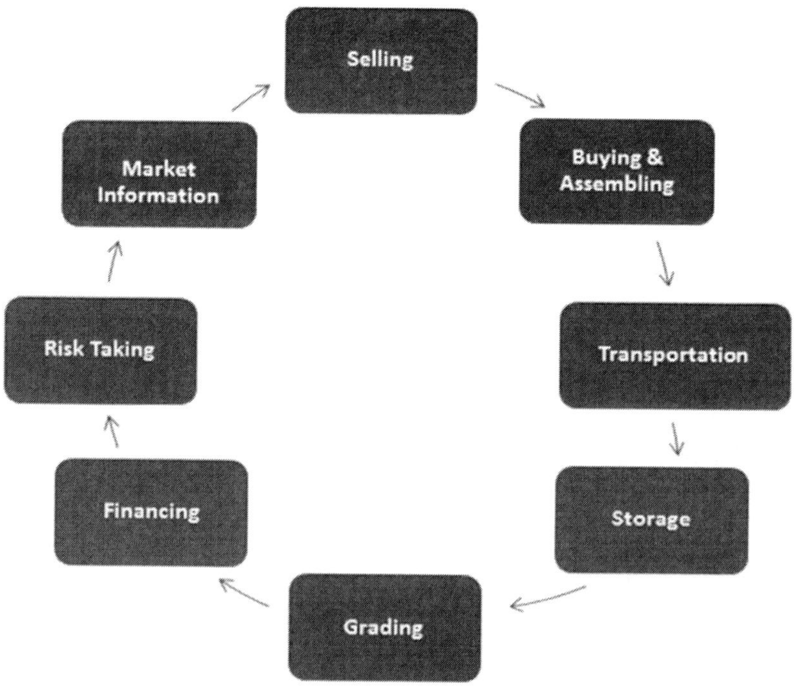

Selling

Selling is the crux of marketing. It involves convincing the prospective buyers to actually complete the purchase of an article. It includes transfer of ownership of products to the buyer.

Selling plays a very vital part in realizing the ultimate aim of earning profit. Selling is groomed by means of personal selling, advertising, publicity and sales promotion. Effectiveness and efficiency in selling determine the volume of the firm's profits and profitability.

Buying and Assembling

It deals with what to buy, of what quality, how much from whom, when and at what price. People in business purchase to increase sales or to decrease costs. Purchasing agents are much tempted by quality, service and price. The products that the retailers buy for resale are selected as per the requirements and preferences of their customers.

Assembling means buying necessary parts and to fit them together to make a product. 'Assembly line' marks a production line made up of purely assembly functions. The assembly operation includes the arrival of individual components at the workplace and issuing of these parts for assembling.

An Assembly line is an arrangement of employees and machines in which each individual has a particular job and the work is passed directly from one employee to the next until the product is complete.

Transportation

Transportation is the physical means through which products are moved from the places where they are produced to those places where they are needed for consumption. It creates locational utility. Transportation is very important from the procurement of raw materials to the delivery of finished products to the

customer's places. Transportation depends mainly on railroads, trucks, waterways, pipelines and airways.

Storage

It includes holding products in proper, i.e., usable or saleable, condition from the time they are produced until they are required by customers in case of finished products or by the production department in case of raw materials and stores.

Storing protects the products from deterioration and helps in carrying over surplus for future consumption or usage in production.

Standardization and Grading

Standardization means setting up certain standards or specifications for products based on the intrinsic physical qualities of any item. This may include quantity like weight and size or quality like colour, shape, appearance, material, taste, sweetness etc. A standard gives rise to uniformity of products.

Grading means classification of standardized items into certain well-defined classes or groups. It includes the division of products into classes made of units possessing similar features of size and quality.

Grading is very essential for raw materials; agricultural products like fruits and cereals; mining products like coal, iron and manganese and forest products like timber.

Financing

Financing involves the application of the capital to meet the financial requirements of agencies dealing with various activities of marketing. The services to ensure the credit and money needed and the costs of getting merchandise into the hands of the final user are mostly referred to as the finance function in marketing. Financing is required for the working capital and fixed capital, which may be secured from three sources – owned capital, bank

loans and advance & trade credit. In other words, different kinds of finances are short-term, medium-term, and long-term finance.

Risk Taking

Risk means loss due to some unforeseen situations. Risk bearing in marketing means the financial risk invested in the ownership of goods held for an anticipated demand, including the possible losses because of a fall in prices and the losses from spoilage, depreciation, obsolescence, fire and floods or any other loss that may occur with the passage of time. They may also be due to decay, deterioration and accidents or due to fluctuation in the prices induced by changes in supply and demand. The different risks are usually termed as place risk, time risk, physical risk, etc.

Market Information

The importance of this facilitating function of marketing has been recently marked. The only sound foundation on which marketing decisions depend is timely and correct market information. The importance of this facilitating function of marketing has been recently marked. The only sound foundation on which marketing decisions depend is timely and correct market information.

7 Ps of Marketing

PRODUCT	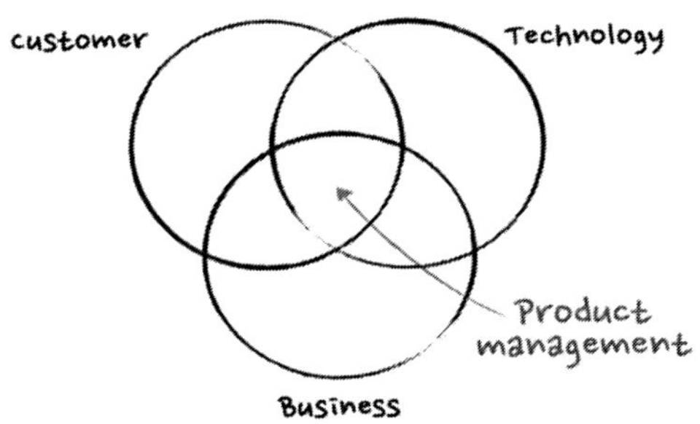

PRICE	
PROMOTION	
PLACE	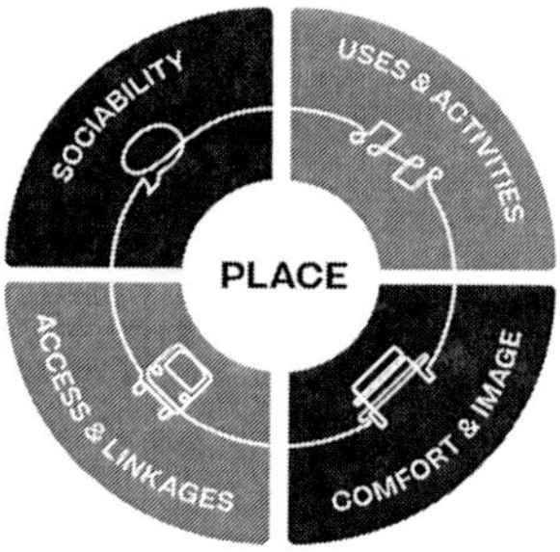
PACKAGING	

POSITIONING	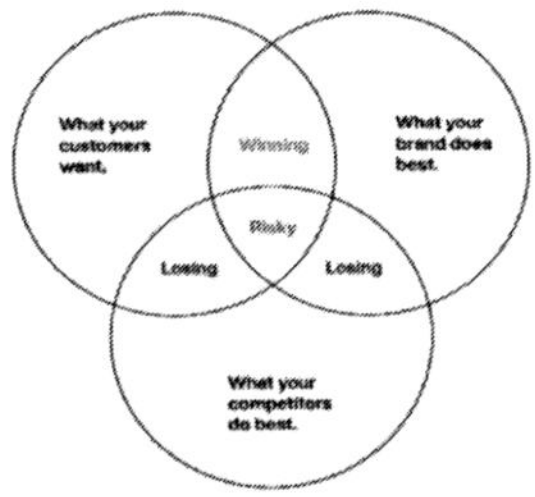
PEOPLE	

Product

To begin with, develop the habit of looking at your product as though you were an outside marketing consultant brought in to help your company decide whether or not it's in the right business at this time. Ask critical questions such as:

- Is your current product or service, or a mix of products and services, appropriate and suitable for the market and the customers of today?

Whenever you're having difficulty selling as many of your products or services as you'd like, you need to develop the habit of assessing your business honestly and asking:

- Are these the right products or services for our customers today?
- Is there any product or service you're offering today that, knowing what you now know, you would not bring out again today?
- Compared to your competitors, is your product or service superior in some significant way to anything else

available? If so, what is it? If not, could you develop an area of superiority?

- Should you be offering this product or service at all in the current marketplace?

Prices

The second P in the formula is price. Develop the habit of continually examining and re-examining the prices of the products and services you sell to make sure they're still appropriate to the realities of the current market. Sometimes you need to lower your prices. At other times, it may be appropriate to raise your prices. Many companies have found that the profitability of certain products or services doesn't justify the amount of effort and resources that go into producing them. By raising their prices, they may lose a percentage of their customers, but the remaining percentage generates a profit on every sale. Could this be appropriate for you? Sometimes you need to change your terms and conditions of sale. Sometimes, by spreading your price over a series of months or years, you can sell far more than you are today, and the interest you can charge will more than makeup for the delay in cash receipts. Sometimes you can combine products and services together with special offers and special promotions. Sometimes you can include free additional items that cost you very little to produce but make your prices appear far more attractive to your customers. In business, as in nature, whenever you experience resistance or frustration in any part of your sales or marketing activities, be open to revisiting that area. Be open to the possibility that your current pricing structure is not ideal for the current market. Be open to the need to revise your prices, if necessary, to remain competitive, to survive and thrive in a fast-changing marketplace.

Promotion

The third habit in marketing and sales is to think in terms of promotion all the time. Promotion includes all the ways you tell

your customers about your products or services and how you then market and sell to them. Small changes in the way you promote and sell your products can lead to dramatic changes in your results. Even small changes in your advertising can lead immediately to higher sales. Experienced copywriters can often increase the response rate from advertising by 500 per cent by simply changing the headline on an advertisement. Large and small companies in every industry continually experiment with different ways of advertising, promoting, and selling their products and services. And here is the rule: Whatever method of marketing and sales you're using today will, sooner or later, stop working. Sometimes it will stop working for reasons you know, and sometimes it will be for reasons you don't know. In either case, your methods of marketing and sales will eventually stop working, and you'll have to develop new sales, marketing and advertising approaches, offerings, and strategies.

Place

The fourth P in the marketing mix is the place where your product or service is actually sold. Develop the habit of reviewing and reflecting upon the exact location where the customer meets the salesperson. Sometimes a change in place can lead to a rapid increase in sales. You can sell your product in many different places. Some companies use direct selling, sending their salespeople out to personally meet and talk with the prospect. Some sell by telemarketing. Some sell through catalogues or mail orders. Some sell at trade shows or in retail establishments. Some sell in joint ventures with other similar products or services. Some companies use manufacturers' representatives or distributors. Many companies use a combination of one or more of these methods. In each case, the entrepreneur must make the right choice about the very best location or place for the customer to receive essential buying information on the product or service needed to make a buying decision. What is yours? In what way should you change it? Where else could you offer your products or services?

Packaging

The fifth element in the marketing mix is the packaging. Develop the habit of standing back and looking at every visual element in the packaging of your product or service through the eyes of a critical prospect. Remember, people form their first impression about you within the first 30 seconds of seeing you or some element of your company. Small improvements in the packaging or external appearance of your product or service can often lead to completely different reactions from your customers. With regard to the packaging of your company, your product or service, you should think in terms of everything that the customer sees from the first moment of contact with your company all the way through the purchasing process. Packaging refers to the way your product or service appears from the outside. Packaging also refers to your people and how they dress and groom. It refers to your offices, your waiting rooms, your brochures, your correspondence and every single visual element of your company. Everything counts. Everything helps or hurts. Everything affects your customer's confidence about dealing with you.

Positioning

The next P is positioning. You should develop the habit of thinking continually about how you are positioned in the hearts and minds of your customers. How do people think and talk about you when you're not present? How do people think and talk about your company? What positioning do you have in your market, in terms of the specific words people use when they describe you and your offerings to others? customers determine how readily they'll buy your product or service and how much they'll pay. Develop the habit of thinking about how you could improve your positioning. Begin by determining the position you'd like to have. If you could create the ideal impression in the hearts and minds of your customers, what would it be? What would you have to do in every customer interaction to

get your customers to think and talk about in that specific way? What changes do you need to make in the way interact with customers today in order to be seen as the very best choice for your customers of tomorrow?

People

The final P of the marketing mix is people. Develop the habit of thinking in terms of the people inside and outside of your business who are responsible for every element of your sales and marketing strategy and activities. It's amazing how many entrepreneurs and businesspeople will work extremely hard to think through every element of the marketing strategy and the marketing mix, and then pay little attention to the fact that every single decision and policy has to be carried out by a specific person, in a specific way. Your ability to select, recruit, hire and retain the proper people, with the skills and abilities to do the job you need to have done, is more important than everything else put together. In his best-selling book, Good to Great, Jim Collins discovered the most important factor applied by the best companies was that they first of all "got the right people on the bus, and the wrong people off the bus." Once these companies had hired the right people, the second step was to "get the right people in the right seats on the bus. "To be successful in business, you must develop the habit of thinking in terms of exactly who is going to carry out each task and responsibility. In many cases, it's not possible to move forward until you can attract and put the right person into the right position. Many of the best business plans ever developed sit on shelves today because the people who created them could not find the key people who could execute those plans.

MARKETING GOAL

Goals are an essential component of your marketing strategy. They are often the place you start. Goals set the direction for what needs to happen for your product or service to do well in the market and are the foundation of the plan you build to get there.

The purpose of marketing is to reach your target audience and communicate the benefits of your product or service – so you can successfully acquire, keep, and grow customers. So, your marketing goals must relate to the specific business objectives your company wants to achieve. A top-down hierarchy of goals keeps your marketing plan aligned with the business strategy and shows the impact of marketing.

Setting focused, realistic, and quantifiable goals upfront establishes a true north for your marketing efforts. This demonstrates the strategic importance of what the team is working on and empowers you to show leadership why your marketing plan is the best approach.

Marketing goal frameworks

Many organizations use a goal management framework to set marketing objectives. Frameworks provide a structured approach for creating relevant and actionable goals. Some of the most popular frameworks include mnemonic devices to help teams remember the elements.

CLEAR goals

Collaborative	Create goals collaboratively to drive momentum and internal buy-in.
Limited	Set goals that are limited in scope and duration.
Emotional	Choose words that make an emotional connection with the team.
Appreciable	Be ready to break large goals down into tactical action items.
Refinable	Be willing to refine and modify your goals in response to new situations and findings.

THE FIVE MARKETING CONCEPTS

The Production Concept

The production concept is focused on operations and is based on the assumption that customers will be more attracted to products that are readily available and can be purchased for less than competing products of the same kind. This concept came about as a result of the rise of early capitalism in the 1950s, at which time, companies were focused on efficiency in manufacturing to ensure maximum profits and scalability. This philosophy can be useful when a company markets in an industry experiencing tremendous growth, but it also carries a risk. Businesses that are overly focused on cheap production can easily lose touch with the needs of the customer and ultimately lose business despite its cheap and accessible goods.

The Product Concept

The product concept is the opposite of the production concept in that it assumes that availability and price don't have a role in customer buying habits and that people generally prefer

quality, innovation, and performance over low cost. Thus, this marketing strategy focuses on continuous product improvement and innovation. Apple Inc. is a prime example of this concept in action. Its target audience always eagerly anticipates the company's new releases. Even though there are off-brand products that perform many of the same functions for a lower price, many folks will not compromise just to save money. Working on this principle alone, however, a marketer could fail to attract those who are also motivated by availability and price.

The Selling Concept

Marketing on the selling concept entails a focus on getting the consumer to the actual transaction without regard for the customer's needs or the product quality – a costly tactic. This concept frequently excludes customer satisfaction efforts and doesn't usually lead to repeat purchases. The selling concept is centred on the belief that you must convince a customer to buy a product through aggressive marketing of the benefits of the product or service because it isn't a necessity. An example is soda pop. Ever wonder why you continue to see ads for Coca Cola despite the prevalence of the brand? Everyone knows what Coke has to offer, but it's widely known that soda lacks nutrients and is bad for your health. Coca Cola knows this, and that's why they spend astonishing amounts of money pushing their product.

The Marketing Concept

The marketing concept is based on increasing a company's ability to compete and achieve maximum profits by marketing the ways in which it offers better value to customers than its competitors. It's all about knowing the target market, sensing its needs, and meeting them most effectively. Many refer to this as the "customer-first approach. "Glossier is a recognizable example of this marketing concept. The company understands that many

women are unhappy with the way that makeup affects the health of their skin. They also noticed that women are fed up with being told what makeup products to use. With this in mind, Glossier introduced a line of skincare and makeup products that not only nourish the skin but are also easy to use and promote individualism and personal expression with makeup.

The Societal Concept

The societal marketing concept is an emerging one that emphasizes the welfare of society. It's based on the idea that marketers have a moral responsibility to market conscientiously to promote what's good for people over what people may want, regardless of a company's sales goals. Employees of a company live in the societies they market to, and they should advertise with the best interests of their local community in mind. The fast-food industry is an example of what the societal concept aims to address. There's a high societal demand for fast food, but this food is high in fat and sugar and contributes to excess waste. Even though the industry is answering the desires of the modern consumer, it's hurting our health and detracting from our society's goal of environmental sustainability.

How to Choose the Right Marketing Concept?

While not all of the above concepts are effective (or perhaps as effective as they once were), you can utilize aspects from multiple concepts in designing and strategizing a marketing plan. As you plan, you need to ask yourself some questions before deciding which marketing concept(s) to base it on. Consider the following:

- Who is your target audience? Which demographics are interested in your products or services? Where are they looking for you and what do you have to offer? What attracts this demographic to your company? How can you use that to turn these people into customers?

- What are your goals besides making money? For example, are you trying to establish a loyal customer base? Are you trying to fill a hole in the industry you're selling in?
- What makes your brand unique? What education do they need to be enticed to buy?

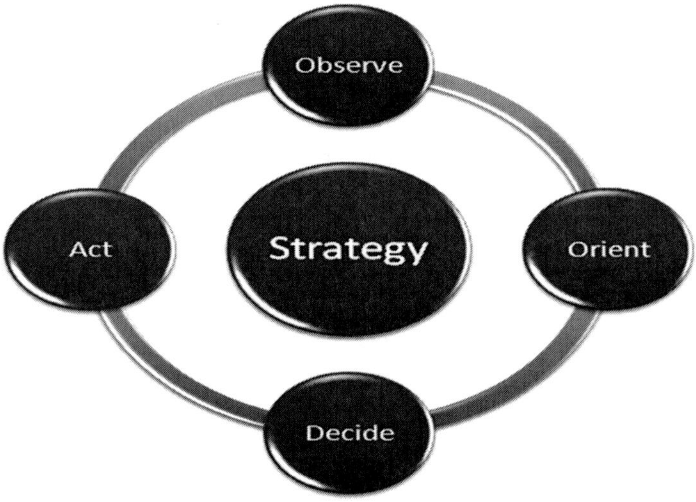

CHAPTER 2

Financial Management

Financial Management is basically concerned with planning, organizing, directing and controlling the financial activities such as procurement and utilisation of funds in an organisation. It is dealing with and analysing money and investments for a person or a business to help make business decisions. Finance is the lifeline of any business. However, finances, like most other resources, are always limited. On the other hand, wants are always unlimited. Therefore, it is important for a business to manage its finances efficiently. Financial management is the centre of activity for all financial managers in a business firm. It is the most important part of management required to look upon during the formation of management strategies for a firm for the acquirement of the desired goal of the firm.

ELEMENTS OF FINANCIAL MANAGEMENT

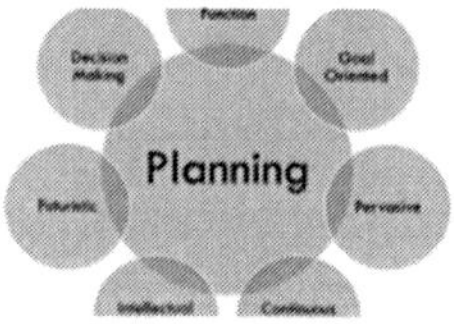

PLANNING

CONTROLLING

ORGANISING

DIRECTING

PLANNING

Planning involves determination of goals as well as the activities required to be undertaken to achieve the goals. In the planning process, managers anticipate the future and accordingly decide what activities must be undertaken.

Key Areas of a Comprehensive Financial Plan

Cash Management

Believe it or not, cash management is the heart and soul of your firm. The computation for firm expenses is actually needed for a smooth run of an organisation. Cash management refers to a broad area of finance involving the collection, handling, and usage of cash.

Effective cash flow management strategies for small businesses

1. Ask for a deposit or milestone payment

Companies whose product or service requires substantial cash or effort before they deliver are good candidates for asking clients for a deposit or milestone payment. Graphic designers, web

designers, marketing agencies, PR agencies and even construction companies fall into this bucket. Not all clients may be willing to make a deposit or milestone payment. The only thing that is guaranteed is that you won't get what you don't ask for. So, encourage your customers to ask their customers for a deposit. That might be just what they need to get on solid footing.

2. Ask customers to pay faster

Another option for managing cash flow is to get customers to pay faster. This can take several forms. The simplest form is to give vendor discounts, where 2/10, Net 30 terms would entail giving customers a 2% discount if the invoice is paid within 10 days. Otherwise, the full amount is due in 30 days. This can be an attractive proposition for a company's customers, as it allows them to make the equivalent of a 73% APR in ten days just by paying their bills faster.

3. Cut or Delay expenses

In the event that customers won't pay faster, another option is to delay expenses. The strategy can take on a variety of forms, depending on the business. Manufacturing companies may consider using lower-cost inputs to deliver the same goods or services, while a service company may opt for spending less time on the same work. Companies should also consider exhausting existing inventory before purchasing new inventory, or hiring part-time or contract employees to replace full-time employees. Also, consider how your client's personal expenses impact their business. Given how much of their expenses may be personal in nature—either indirectly via the salary they pay themselves, or directly as a sole proprietor—they might want to consider what opportunities they have to cut back on their personal expenses. It may entail eating out less, downsizing, living more frugally or delaying a vacation. Out of all the variables listed here, personal expenses are the ones business owners have the most direct control over.

4. Request more favourable payment terms from vendors

As they value their clients, vendors have a strong incentive to help finance their customers' purchases. Getting an extra two weeks to make a payment could be the difference between missing payroll and expanding. If your payment terms are 15 days, ask for 30 days. If they are 30 days, ask for 45 days. Depending on your relationship with your vendors, you'll find that at least some will be open to a more favourable arrangement. And, be persistent! Perhaps you've tried asking for more favourable payments terms before but were declined. You have little to lose by asking again, either inquiring from the same vendor or a different vendor. Of course, the timelier and more dependable you are with them, the more willing they will be to extend their terms.

5. Finance purchase orders

For manufacturing or merchandising companies that require a significant amount of cash to fulfil their purchase orders, financing purchase orders could be a solution. Once you have a purchase order on hand, the financing company will pay the vendor so you can get the merchandise or inventory the company needs to fulfil the purchase order. This eliminates the problem of getting a large order, but not being able to fulfil it because of cash to buy the inventory or materials.

6. Increase margins

Increasing its margins will help a business spin off more cash that can be used to fund operations. The only two ways a business can increase its margin are by increasing what it charges or decreasing the cost to deliver the product or service. Neither of these may be feasible for a majority of businesses. However, raising prices is a real option for businesses with strong demand for their product or service, or with a unique product, offering or value proposition that is not available from competitors. Any increase in prices will have to be positioned carefully to avoid alienating customers.

7. Sell or lease idle equipment

When cash is tight, everything should be on the table. This is especially true of idle equipment that can be sold for cash or leased to another company that can put it to use. Even if the company is using the equipment, it should consider that the same equipment could be rented for much less, while the proceeds from the sale can be used to fund the business in the interim. This especially makes sense for long-lived equipment that is easy to move, transport or install. If you have a storage centre with equipment, you'll also be saving on storage costs. With Craigslist, chances are, you'll be able to pick up the same equipment at a later time for a fraction of the cost.

8. Sell future revenue

A merchant cash advance is a viable strategy for consumer businesses like retailers and restaurants. It involves taking a loan that is automatically repaid via a percentage of the credit and debit card transaction volume received by the business. This strategy is especially viable for businesses with strong transaction history. Just make sure that the company's margins can support the cost of the financing. Otherwise, they could be paving their way to financial ruin.

9. Turn down, shift or postpone work

Managing cash flow is as much about timing as anything. Getting a year's worth of business in one month is overwhelming for most businesses. On the flip side, insufficient business could mean shutting the doors. Thus, managing the volume of business for consistency can be a helpful way to manage cash flow. This may entail turning down or postponing work at certain times of the year. This strategy is not realistic for companies with strongly seasonal businesses. Retailers, snowblowers and tax accountants will not be able to change the seasonality of their business. However, many other companies and industries do have the ability to better

plan for more consistent volume and shift the timing of the work. Think win-win. For instance, you can offer good clients a discount for postponing their work, order or service.

10. Sell invoices

Selling invoices, also known as invoice factoring, invoice discounting, invoice financing, etc., is a very flexible and quick form of business funding available for B2B companies. In a nutshell, invoices are assets of a company. The product or service has been completed and delivered, but the cash is locked up in the invoice until the customer pays. Factoring can be a solution when payment terms are 15, 30 or even 60 days. Instead of waiting 60 days for the client to pay, a company can "sell" the invoice to a factoring company and get money upfront. 60 days later, the client pays off the invoice, so the company never had to take on any debt. Here is a great post about the basics of invoice factoring, and what to look for in a funding provider.

Investment Planning

Investment planning is more than just buying and selling securities. Nowadays, even robots can do that. What makes a human advisor irreplaceable is our knowledge to interpret and adjust to new laws and regulations to your advantage. Furthermore, financial planners can help you find the right financial tools to meet your unique needs.

Tax Management

Tax management refers to the management of finances, for the purpose of paying taxes. Tax Management deals with filing Returns in time, getting the accounts audited, deducting tax at source etc. Tax Management helps in avoiding payment of interest, penalty, and prosecution. Getting a comprehensive financial plan is similar to getting comprehensive blood work done when you first visit your primary doctor. Subsequently, any

enzyme levels that deviate from your initial normal level would indicate a need for further study and analysis. The same is true with your comprehensive financial plan. Without the initial plan, you'll be clueless about your progress or missed opportunities.

Comprehensive financial planning provides a clear picture of your current financial profile and it aids the planner tremendously to strategize and offer guidance for your future. Moreover, planning should be adjusted and evolve with you as your goals and financial status change.

CONTROLLING

Control is a function of management that helps to check errors in order to take corrective actions. This is done to minimize deviation from standards and ensure that the stated goals of the organization are achieved in the desired manner.

For example, if a sales manager makes a target to make sales of 5 million in one quarter with five salespersons working in his team, then he will give the target of 1 million to every salesperson and will control their actions to achieve the desired results.

PROCESS OF CONTROLLING

1. Formation of standards

The first step of the controlling process is the formation of standards. The manager first prepares a report stating the standards expected from the project given to employees. The standards are not decided by randomly picking a figure, but it is decided on the basis of the past performance of employees and performance of last season and the condition of the market. Before revealing the expected standards to employees and giving them the target, the standards are approved by the senior management. After getting the approval of the management, these standards are discussed with the team members, and the target is given to each team member. A pre-formed standard gives a common goal to employees to work towards.

2. Measurement of actual performance

Once the task is completed, it is the job of the manager to measure the performance of the employees. The manager will analyse the performance of each employee and ask them to submit their report of work.

3. Comparison of actual performance with the standard performance

After the measurement of the actual report, a comparison is made between the actual performance and the pre-decided standard performance and the difference is calculated between both the performances and a report is generated after the analysis of the performance of all employees.

4. Taking corrective actions if required

After comparing the standard performance with the actual performance of employees. The difference is calculated. Then the performance of each employee is analysed, and the difference between the target given to them and the percentage of target achieved by them is observed, and the required actions are taken as per the policy of the company and the past performance of the employee.

ORGANISING

Organising is the process of identifying and grouping the work to be performed, defining and delegating responsibility and authority, and establishing relationships for the purpose of enabling people to work most effectively together in accomplishing objectives. Organising is the establishment of effective authority relationships among selected works, persons and workplaces in order for the group to work together efficiently, or the process of dividing work into sections and departments.

Common Elements of Organizations

Organizational psychologist Edgar Schein proposes four common elements of an organization's structure From a manager's

point of view, operations are made successful by instilling a common purpose to create a coordinated effort across the organization and organizing resources based on tasks and decision making. Each of the four elements is relatively straightforward in theory but represents a critical component of an effective structure.

Edgar Schein speaking about corporate culture:

Common Purpose

An organization without a clear purpose or mission soon begins to drift and become disorganized. A common purpose unifies employees or members and gives everyone an understanding of the organization's direction. Ensuring that the common purpose is effectively communicated across organizations (particularly large organizations with many moving parts) is a central task for managers. Managers communicate this purpose by educating all employees on the general strategy, mission statement, values, and short- and long-term objectives of the organization.

Coordinated Effort

The coordinating effort involves working together in a way that maximizes resources. The common purpose is achieved through the coordinated effort of all individuals and groups within an organization. The broader group's diverse skill sets and personalities must be leveraged in a way that adds value. The act of coordinating organizational effort is perhaps the most important responsibility of managers because it motivates and distributes human resources to capture value.

Division of Labour

Division of labour is also known as work specification for greater efficiency. It involves delegating specific parts of a broader task to different people within the organization based on their particular abilities and skills. Using division of labour, an organization can

parcel out a complex work effort for specialists to perform. By systematically dividing complex tasks into specialized jobs, an organization uses its human resources more efficiently.

Hierarchy of Authority

The hierarchy of authority is essentially the chain of command–a control mechanism for making sure the right people do the right things at the right time. While there are a wide variety of organizational structures–some with more centralization of authority than others–hierarchy in decision making is a critical factor for success. Knowing who will make decisions under what circumstances enables organizations to be agile, while the ambiguity of authority can often slow the decision-making process. Authority enables organizations to set directions and select strategies, which can, in turn, enable a common purpose.

Characteristics of Organizational Structures

Span of Control

The span of control–or the number of subordinates a supervisor has–is used as a means of ensuring proper coordination and a sense of accountability among employees. It determines the number of levels of management an organization has as well as the number of employees a manager can efficiently and effectively manage. In the execution of a task, hierarchical organizations usually have different levels of task processes. Workers at various levels send reports on their progress to the next levels until the work is completed.

Departmentalization

Departmentalization is the process of grouping individuals into departments and grouping departments into total organizations. Different approaches include:

Functional - departmentalization by common skills and work tasks

Divisional - departmentalization by common product, program, or geographical location

Matrix - a complex combination of functional and divisional

Team - departmentalization by teams of people brought together to accomplish specific tasks

Network - independent departments providing functions for a central core breaker

Centralization

Centralization occurs when decision-making authority is located in the upper organizational levels. Centralization increases consistency in the processes and procedures that employees use in performing tasks. In this way, it promotes workplace harmony among workers and reduces the cost of production. Centralization is usually helpful when an organization is in crisis and/or faces the risk of failure. Centralization allows for rapid, department-wide decision-making; there is also less duplication of work because fewer employees perform the same task. However, it can limit flexibility and natural synergies. Autonomy in decision-making is reserved for only a small number of individuals within the workforce, potentially limiting creativity.

DIRECTING

Directing is the heart of management function. All other functions of management such as planning, organizing, and staffing have no importance without directing. Leadership, motivation, supervision, and communication are various aspects of directing. Directing refers to a process or technique of instructing, guiding, inspiring, counselling, overseeing and leading people towards the accomplishment of organizational goals. It is a continuous managerial process that goes on throughout the life of the organization.

Four Steps to Setting Direction and Pace - Management Essentials

The four-step approach is as follows:

Set goals

First, you need to set a team goal that supports organizational goals. Goals don't need to be expressed in measurable terms; in fact, goals are typically stated in abstract and general terms. They do need to support the organization's overall mission, vision, and values. Involving your team members in developing a goal will give them a sense of ownership and increase their commitment to achieving the goal.

Create objectives

In line with the goals set for the team, you need to create objectives to make sure the team achieves those goals. Objectives must be measurable so that progress can be tracked. You should use the SMART model, ensuring that the objectives you set are specific, measurable, achievable, realistic, and time-bound.

Define a plan of action

Once you've set goals and objectives, you have to specify what must be done to accomplish them. This is the action plan for your team. An action plan identifies the tasks and deliverables that must be completed to achieve objectives, which in turn enable the team to achieve its goals. You must also provide direction in the form of targets and timelines. At a team level, it's really the action plan that sets direction and pace. Define a new action plan for each budget period to ensure that your team's work is aligned with the goals and vision of the organization.

Follow up

After providing direction in the form of an action plan, you need to monitor progress. This is the purpose of the final step

of following up. You need to ensure that what's laid out in the plan is being achieved. If necessary, modify the action plan to get progress back on track or to reflect changes made at higher levels of the organization. During the follow-up step, you can also evaluate the overall performance of the team and the effectiveness of its goals and objectives, and provide feedback and encouragement to keep team members on track.

Elements or Techniques of Direction

There are various elements involved in direction are as follows:-

1. Issuing Orders and Instructions to Subordinates

The first and foremost element of direction is to issue orders and instructions which are considered an essential step in the process of directing subordinates. An order is a fundamental tool for getting things done. Therefore, the orders and instructions reflect managerial decisions and initiate action on the part of subordinates. Orders may be general or specific, formal or informal, written or oral.

Thus, an order should serve the following characteristics:

- The order should be clear and complete.
- It should be reasonable and attainable.
- The order must be in tune with the various other objectives of the organization and also for the interests of the subordinates.
- All orders should follow the chain of command.
- Face-to-face suggestions are preferable to long distance orders.

2. Supervision in an overall manner

It refers to monitoring the progress of routine work of one's subordinates and guiding them properly. Supervision is an important element of the directing function of management.

Supervision has an important feature which includes face-to-face interaction between the supervisor and his subordinates.

It involves direct personal contact with subordinates. Supervision converts plans into action. Thus supervision is considered an essential step in the process of directing.

3. Motivating Subordinates

The term motivation can be referred to as that process that excites people to work for the attainment of the desired objective. Among the various factors of production, it is only the human factor that is dynamic and provides mobility to other physical resources.

Thus, in an overall sense, it becomes essential so as to motivate the human resources so as to keep the employees dynamic, aware and eager to perform their duty. Both monetary and non-monetary incentives are given to the employees for motivation. Thus, through motivation, the employees will perform better. Hence, it will help to achieve the organizational goals and objectives.

4. Providing Leadership

The term Leadership defines as influencing others in such a manner as to guide them to do what the leader wants them to do. Leadership plays an important role in directing. Only through this leadership skill, a manager can develop trust and zeal among his subordinates. Therefore, it leads to guide and provide overall counselling to subordinates in the best way for achieving their objectives and also for the organization.

5. Communicating with Subordinates

It refers to an act of transferring facts, ideas, feeling, etc. from one person to another and making him understand them. A

manager has to continuously guide and also at the same time monitor his subordinates about what to do, how to do, and when to do various things.

Also, it is very essential to know their reactions. To do all this it becomes essential to develop effective telecommunication facilities. Therefore, the essential feature is to communicate as developing mutual understanding inculcates a sense of cooperation which builds an environment of coordination in the organization.

6. Maintaining discipline and Rewarding Effective People

By maintaining an atmosphere of discipline and trust in the organization, the manager can easily give directions. So that the work is done by his employees in the most efficient and effective manner. In return, the employees will get a reward in the form of bonuses, incentives and other perks so as to get themselves associated with the organization on a long-term basis. Therefore, this element of direction also plays a very important role in achieving the overall objectives of an organization.

Types of Financial Decisions in Financial Management

Everything you need to know about the types of financial decisions taken by a company. The key aspects of financial decision-making relate to financing, investment, dividends and working capital management.

Decision making helps to utilise the available resources for achieving the objectives of the organization, unless minimum financial performance levels are achieved, it is impossible for a business enterprise to survive over time.

Therefore, financial management basically provides a conceptual and analytical framework for financial decision making.

There are four main financial decisions:-

1. Capital Budgeting or Long-term Investment Decision

2. Capital Structure or Financing Decision
3. Dividend Decision
4. Working Capital Management Decision.

Types of Financial Decisions: Investment Decision, Financing Decision, Dividend Decision and Working Capital Management Decision

Types of Financial Decisions - That Every Company is Required to Take: Investment Decision, Financing Decision and Dividend Decision

Every company is required to take three main financial decisions, they are:

1. Investment Decision
2. Financing Decision
3. Dividend Decision

1. Investment Decision:

A financial decision is concerned with how the firm's funds are invested in different assets is known as an investment decision. An investment decision can be long-term or short-term. A long-term investment decision is called a capital budgeting decision which involves huge amounts of long-term investments and is irreversible except at a huge cost. Short-term investment decisions are called working capital decisions, which affect day to day working of a business. It includes the decisions about the levels of cash, inventory and receivables. A bad capital budgeting decision normally has the capacity to severely damage the financial fortune of a business. A bad working capital decision affects the liquidity and profitability of a business.

Factors Affecting Investment Decisions / Capital Budgeting Decisions:

1. Cash flows of the project- The series of cash receipts and payments over the life of an investment proposal should be considered and analyzed for selecting the best proposal.

2. Rate of return- The expected returns from each proposal and risk involved in them should be taken into account to select the best proposal.

3. Investment criteria involved- The various investment proposals are evaluated on the basis of capital budgeting techniques. Which involve calculation regarding investment amount, interest rate, cash flows, rate of return etc. It is to be considered which technique to use for evaluation of projects.

2. Financing Decision:

A financial decision is concerned with the amount of finance to be raised from various long-term sources of funds like equity shares, preference shares, debentures, bank loans etc. In other words, it is a decision on the 'capital structure' of the company.

Capital Structure Owner's Fund + Borrowed Fund

Financial Risk:

The risk of default on the payment of periodical interest and repayment of capital on 'borrowed funds' is called financial risk.

Factors Affecting Financing Decision:

1. Cost- The cost of raising funds from different sources is different. The cost of equity is more than the cost of debts. The cheapest source should be selected prudently.

2. Risk- The risk associated with different sources is different. More risk is associated with borrowed funds as compared to the owner's fund as interest is paid on it and it is also repaid after a fixed period of time or on the expiry of its tenure.

3. Flotation cost- The cost involved in issuing securities such as broker's commission, underwriter's fees, expenses on prospectus etc. Is called flotation cost. The higher the flotation cost, the less attractive is the source of finance.

4. Cash flow position of the business- In case the cash flow position of a company is good enough then it can easily use borrowed funds.

5. Control considerations- In case the existing shareholders want to retain complete control of the business then finance can be raised through borrowed funds but when they are ready for dilution of control over the business, equity shares can be used for raising finance.

6. State of capital markets- During the boom period, finance can easily be raised by issuing shares but during the depression period, raising finance by means of debt is easy.

3. Dividend Decision:

A financial decision is concerned with deciding how much of the profit earned by the company should be distributed among shareholders (dividend) and how much should be retained for future contingencies (retained earnings) is called a dividend decision.

A dividend refers to that part of the profit which is distributed to shareholders. The decision regarding dividends should be taken keeping in view the overall objective of maximizing shareholders' wealth.

Factors affecting Dividend Decision:

1. Earnings- A company having high and stable earnings could declare a high rate of dividends as dividends are paid out of the current and past earnings.

2. Stability of dividends- Companies generally follow the policy of stable dividends. The dividend per share is not altered in case the earnings change by a small proportion or the increase in earnings is temporary in nature.

3. Growth prospects- In case there are growth prospects for the company in the near future then, it will retain its earnings and thus, no or less dividend will be declared.

4. Cash flow positions- Dividends involve an outflow of cash and thus, the availability of adequate cash is the foremost requirement for the declaration of dividends.

5. Preference of shareholders- While deciding about dividends the preference of shareholders is also taken into account. In case shareholders desire for dividend then the company may go for declaring the same. In such case the amount of dividend depends upon the degree of expectations of shareholders.

6. Taxation policy- A company is required to pay tax on dividend declared by it. If the tax on dividends is higher, the company will prefer to pay less by way of dividends whereas if tax rates are lower, then more dividends can be declared by the company.

Chapter 3

Sales Management

Sales management is the process of hiring, motivating and sales staff as well as coordinating sales operations and implementing sales techniques that allow a business to consistently succeed, and even surpass, its sales targets over a year. The process of developing, planning, monitoring, and controlling the entire process of selling your company's goods or services. It also concerns recruiting, training, and supervising your sales force and covers all pre-sales, sales, and post-sales activities.

Sales management components:

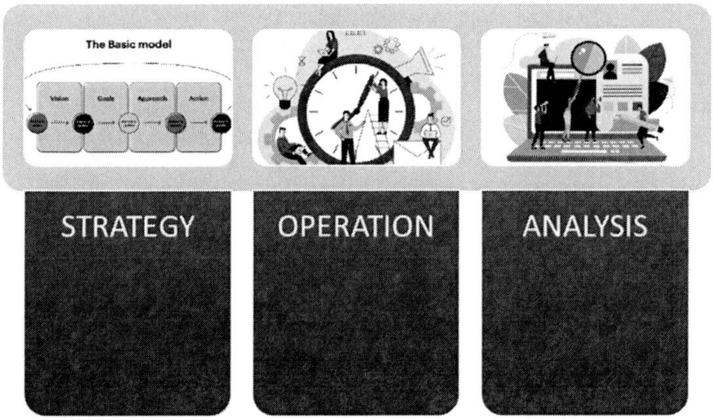

STRATEGY:

Without having a clear strategy your sales efforts will be inefficacious. To know what resources and specialists your business may require, you should set up a sales process and plan a series of activities at every stage of your sales funnel or sales pipeline. This can be done for either the whole company or in regard to individual brands, goods, or services.

Sales funnel

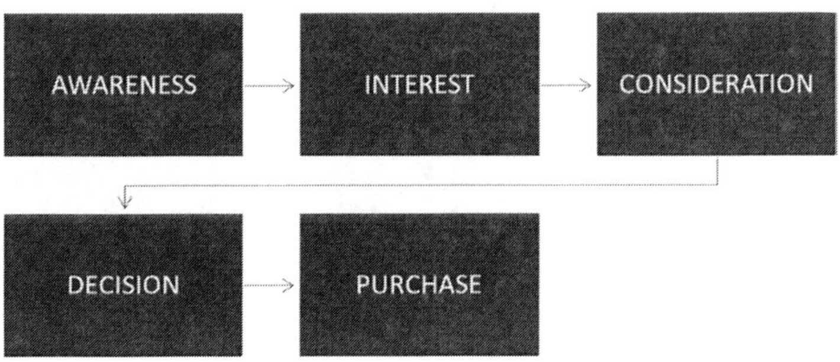

A sales funnel is a powerful analytical tool, if designed with a data-first approach. It describes a single customer's journey

through 5 steps: awareness, interest, consideration, decision, and – the most desired stage for all businesses – purchase.

Stage 1: Awareness

The first of the sales funnel stages is called the "awareness" level because it's where people first become aware of your product or service. They may hear about you from your advertising, social media, and even word of mouth. How and why those people move down the sales funnel depends on your own sales and marketing ability, of course. The leads in the middle and lower sales funnel stages are those that you want to pay the most attention to because they've moved beyond awareness to interest. An example of the awareness stage would be a prospect learning about your company for the first time. Perhaps they clicked on one of your ads, read your blog, found your website via a Google search, or heard a colleague talking about your product or service.

Stage 2: Interest

Once prospects have learned about your brand, they'll evaluate it based on their interest level. They'll think about the problem they're trying to solve and conduct competitive research to make sure your offering is the best solution.

Stage 3: Consideration

Present all sorts of information regarding your product/service. Showing videos, case studies, trials, and webinars will help in knowing the customer about the product/service in detail and judging.

Stage 4: Decision

Off trial demos, new customer discounts, anything that will make your prospect put your product in the cart and press checkout.

Stage 5: Purchase

Provide personalised attention, emails with valuable onboarding content, good customer service and a regular newsletter so the

customer doesn't feel neglected after the sale. This can turn the customer into a loyal brand.

The funnels conditions sales pipeline – determined stages of reaching out to clients. It varies between companies, depending on the market type, resources owned, and business objectives. But as a rule, the pipeline has such stages as lead generation, qualification, meeting, proposal, and closing the deal. Keeping in mind the funnel and the pipeline, you'll be able to come up with a documented sales plan. This typically covers:

Development goals

Sales Key performance indicator

Buyer personas profiles

People and processes

Exact selling methodologies

Software needed

2. Operations

A sophisticated strategy isn't worth a penny without being implemented. You need the team on paper to come true. People are the stumbling block that separates average companies from the best players in the market.

It's not only that sales reps bring you revenue – they are your brand's ambassadors. Salespeople directly deal with:

Lead conversion. They build a bridge between what the client needs and what your company can offer.

Business growth. Sales representatives initialize referrals and help build customer loyalty.

Client retention. Their connections with customers shouldn't be under-evaluated. Remember that a 5% increase in retention rates may boost profits by 25%.

3. Analysis

Sales analysis concerns either KPIs and sales metrics. A key point here is to bring actionable insights that can be further used in the sales strategy. The following effectiveness indicators are usually used by most sales managers:

Total revenue

Revenue growth rate

Revenue distribution by sources

Revenue distribution by representatives

Average conversion rate

Sales-to-date

Average purchase value.

Sales management process

1. Hire a Team

If you're building a sales team from scratch, the best place to start is with your customers.

- What does their buying process like?

- How many people are involved in making the purchasing decision?

- What obstacles might those decision-makers encounter during their journey?

You'll then want to look at your business strategy to determine how buyer goals align with your organizational objectives.

Once you've established some criteria around who your ideal customer is and how your sales process aligns with your big-picture goals, you'll want to then come up with a job description that clearly defines the responsibilities that come with the territory and how they align with your big-picture goals.

We also recommend including information about your company–particularly your organization's mission and values–as this can help attract candidates that align with those core values.

Sales have a notoriously high turnover rate so making sure you find the right people is essential for putting together a team that sticks around for the long haul.

2. Establish Compensation Structure

Before you publish a job posting, you'll want to develop a clearly-defined compensation plan. After all, most reps aren't going to accept a job until they know how much money they'll be making. A compensation plan should include base pay, commission, and other incentives they may be eligible for based on their performance.

Remember, the goal of a compensation plan is to encourage positive behaviours that drive results for your company.

Factors to consider as you put together your compensation structure:

- What's your budget?
- How much do your competitors offer their reps?
- What are your organizational goals?

In a recent post, we broke down eight types of commission structures, weighing the pros, cons, and when to use each one. We also mention that more money doesn't always lead to better performance.

3. Set Targets

Sales targets represent the number of sales or amount of revenue that a sales manager determines a rep should hit within a specific amount of time. In other words, how much money do you expect reps to bring in each month/quarter/year? Make sure you set realistic targets by looking at your current average close rate as a starting point. From there, you'll want to determine how much each rep needs to sell to maintain that average, then set the bar a bit higher. For example, if each rep needs to close 10 deals to break even, you might set the quota at 15, giving you a bit of wiggle room.

That said, avoid setting targets too high, you want to keep sellers motivated by challenging them and setting them up for success.

4. Establish Goals and KPIs (Key performing indicators)

Key performance indicators (KPIs) track your performance against your business goals. To set the stage for success, you'll need to determine which KPIs are most relevant to your industry and strategic goals, as focusing on the wrong metrics can actively damage your brand and bottom line.

Common KPIs include:

- Conversion rates
- Average sales cycle length
- Number of deals in the pipeline
- Pipeline value
- MQL to SQL conversion rate
- Customer lifetime value
- Sales by territory

The list goes on, however, the key thing to keep in mind here is that the KPIs you choose should come together to help you track progress toward a specific goal-otherwise, they're just vanity metrics.

5. Build A Sales Stack

You'll want to enable your sales team with the right tools for getting the job done. Tools vary by organization and are determined by a number of factors including whether your reps do inside or outside sales, how many territories you sell to, whether you work with affiliates or network partners, etc. That said, on a basic level, technology should generally support the activities associated with each pipeline stage.

6. Assign Territories

You'll want to make sure you place top-performers in your most profitable regions to maximize revenue. At the same time, you'll also want to ensure that all reps have enough prospects

and leads to work with, and that their territories don't overlap with other sellers. We explain it in more detail here, but territory mapping allows sales leaders to ensure reps cover the right areas, demographics, and ideal prospects.

7. Choose A Model

First, you'll want to choose a model for your sales management process. There are three common models, which break down as follows:

Island

The island leaves sellers largely on their own, with minimal structure, and a handful of basic tech and information they need to do their job. Traditionally, the island approach is relatively hands-off and is more competitive than collaborative. While some reps thrive in this environment, and it's easy to attribute wins to individuals, it's also really challenging to ensure that reps stick to the script.

Assembly line

The assembly line model is a team-based model where each rep specializes in a specific part of the sales cycle. For example, some reps focus on lead generation, others handle prospecting, presentations, or swoop in at the end to close the deal. The benefit here is, the assembly line allows reps to really master a specific set of skills, it's easy to identify and fix problems, and it can be a really efficient way to get results. At the same time, it requires a large team and can contribute to silos and inconsistent experiences, as buyers deal with different people at different stages in the process.

Pod

In the "pod" model, the sales force is divided into a series of small teams or pods. Each pod is assigned a specific customer type. The pod is similar to the assembly line approach, as each rep

is assigned to a particular stage in the sales process. The difference is that the pod approach is more customer-centric and focuses on developing a team of close-knit, highly-specialized sellers who work exclusively with a single customer segment. This model works best for organizations with long sales cycles, particularly those that follow an account-based marketing approach.

8. Set Territories

Okay, we already mentioned territory assignments, but you'll want to revisit this area as you develop your strategy. This time around, you'll want to make sure you get the most from your resources. Use territory management software to identify viable accounts in each reps' territory, optimize meeting schedules and routes, and redesign territories to keep pipelines topped up.

9. Forecast Performance

Sales forecasting is the process of estimating future sales based on historical data. More specifically, forecasting refers to the ability to predict what the sales team, individual, or company will sell weekly, quarterly, or annually. Sales managers use sales forecasts to anticipate how much revenue their team will bring in over a certain period, as well as identify potential issues in advance. That way, organizations can come up with a contingency plan to mitigate potential damage to the bottom line. For example, if you find that your team is trending 20% below their sales targets, you can do some digging to find out what went wrong and take action.

Maybe your competitor has started an aggressive new discounting campaign, your sales team is wasting time looking for content to send buyers, or your compensation plan doesn't inspire much action. The ability to unearth these types of problems early on can save your organization from major losses down the line and prevent sellers from developing bad habits that get in their way. Forecasting also factors into a number of critical decisions from resource planning to budgeting, quota-setting, and hiring new talent.

10. Track Activity Metrics

Sales activity metrics reveal what salespeople are doing on a daily basis and typically include the following:

- Number of leads created
- Number of emails sent
- Number of calls made
- Number of meetings booked
- Number of conversations with prospects
- Number of social media interactions
- Number of proposals sent
- Number of demo presentations

Keep in mind, activity metrics are often misused and misunderstood. As a manager, you'll need to make sure that you clearly define these "what" and "how many" metrics in a way that drives the outcomes you're looking for.

11. Develop Essential Sales Skills

Coaching and developing the sales team is increasingly becoming a more important part of any sales manager's job. Leaders must model effective sales techniques and help reps overcome weaknesses. Ongoing training should focus on sharpening critical sales skills like prospecting and giving a demo, as well as building on existing knowledge.

12. Improve the Customer Experience

As sales become increasingly customer-centric, sellers must learn to present tailored solutions to each prospect. Your training program should focus on how to identify buyer-specific needs and help them achieve their goals at each stage in the pipeline. While sales leaders can't control the execution of these activities, they can look at individual productivity metrics and outcomes. Then

from there, they might use those insights to develop individual improvement plans. For a deeper dive into activity metrics and their role in the sales process, check out this recent post.

Effective sales management tactics

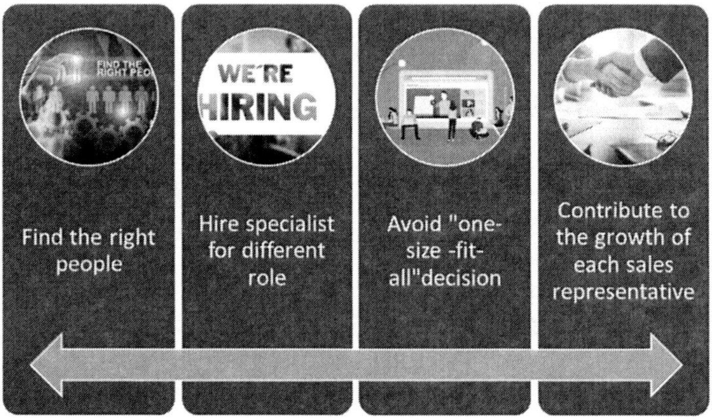

1. Find the right people

Of course, staffing is a responsibility of the HR department. But for the manager, it's crucial to translate vision and requirements to future employees to hire the right people.

The "right" doesn't mean "the best", though. Don't look for Jack of all trades. Overloaded job descriptions are not effective.

2. Avoid "one-size-fits-all" decisions

Whatever you manage, people or processes, avoid oversimplification and too much extrapolation. What works in a crisis may not work when the growth starts, and vice versa. Be flexible and an out-of-the-box thinker.

3. Hire specialists for different roles

If your business grows, you'll have to divide responsibilities. One employee can't combine several roles. As soon as you feel your workers can't cope with the amount of work and tasks they get – hire more professionals.

4. Contribute to the growth of each sales representative

Best salespeople bring your company the most deals thanks to their experience, personal qualities, luck, or all three at a time. But if the team's imbalance grows rapidly, you get a lot of deferred risks:

Inner tension

Loss of motivation

Irreplaceable employees

The manager's task here is to understand why one sales rep performs much better than others and stabilize the situation. This is not about equalizing all, this is about finding points of growth for every team member.

The 5 Most Successful Sales Strategies

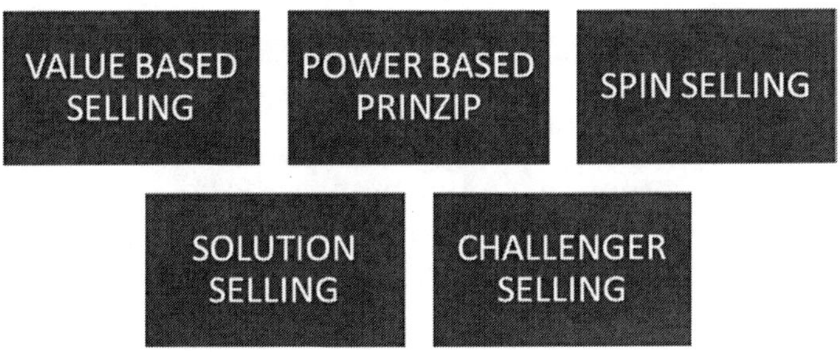

1. Value-Based Selling: Demonstrating the product value with the customer example

As the name implies, this sales method is based on the value your customer experiences with the use of your product. At the beginning of the relationship, the salesperson collects as much information about the customer as possible. It is important to take a close look at the customer's business model in advance and drill deep into the details of everything they say.

Even two seemingly identical companies operating in the same industry may have developed completely different strategies on how to address and solve their problems. This often results in different

pricing models, sales models and cost structures. If you have identified at least one challenge or pain in the product or company that you can help to solve, you have a strong reason to talk to the prospect.

This sales approach is particularly exciting if you sell a highly customizable product. Then it is possible to adapt it exactly to the needs of the customer. Such products are often accompanied by comparatively high price models. That's why the sales employee should pay particular attention to really understanding the customer's needs in value-based selling. This helps the salesperson in advanced discussions, even during price negotiations. At the end of the process, the product price is in turn compared with the value delivered to the customer. The higher this value is and the more clearly it is presented, the better the price negotiations will go and the more likely it is that a contract will be signed.

2. The Power-Base Principle: Industry knowledge is king

The next sales strategy highlighted here is the power base principle. Here, the sales employee assumes an expert or consultant role. He is then in a particularly strong position, namely in the "power base". The prerequisite for this is, of course, that the salesperson has enough experience or expertise in the respective field. Prospects buy from salespeople they trust so nothing is worse than being thought of as untrustworthy by the prospect. Authenticity stands above all else with this method. With the power base principle, the salesperson knows the customer's target market better than the customer themselves. Being able to hold technically and professionally in-depth discussions, the salesperson brings in their expertise and then develops a business strategy together with the customer.

The close contact between the decision-maker and "consultant" also helps the salesperson to stay ahead of the game in follow-up projects. The higher the complexity of the product or service and the complexity of the customer target market, the more effective the power base principle is.

3. SPIN Selling: By asking questions about emotional attachment

This method of direct selling puts a heavy focus on the questioning of the customer. The aim of this sales strategy is to build up the most emotional bond with the dialogue partner in order to set the exit hurdle from the sales process as high as possible.

SPIN distinguishes between four question types:

- Situational questions, in order to get to know the general conditions and situation of the customer.
- Problem questions to identify concrete challenges and pains of the customer to understand how to place the solution to be the most applicable solution.
- Implication questions, which are used to identify or create the biggest problem in order to present oneself later as a contact person for problem solving.
- Need-payoff questions to determine the value to the customer that the problem solution would create. In a sense, SPIN Selling is the predecessor of Solution Selling. In Solution Selling, the gaining of information is further deepened by asking specific questions. Since Solution Selling extends the SPIN approach, I recommend that you no longer apply SPIN Selling separately but embed it in your Solution Selling.

4. Solution Selling: Solving problems instead of just selling

One sales strategy that is currently highly regarded is solution selling. More and more companies are moving away from pure product sales and towards solution selling. The reason for this is very simple: Customers are becoming more demanding and can usually find out about mere product information and price themselves via the Internet. If the added value or unique selling proposition is not sufficiently clear, there is a risk that the potential customer will decide on the basis of price alone. It is therefore not only important for the

sales representative to present the advantages of his product. Rather, they are required to deal with the business challenges of their potential customer, similar to value-based selling. As a rule, the salesperson and customer first work out the existing challenges and develop potential solutions in a workshop-like discussion. In solution selling, the seller offers the potential customer significantly more than just providing a product. Often the presentation consists of planning, consulting, recommendations for use and regular training. The result is a complete package for the customer whose added value goes far beyond that of the actual product. Solution selling is often used for products that are sold in both the high-price and low-price segments. This is one of the reasons why solution selling usually includes a return-on-investment or amortization calculation. It is important here that the figures on which the cost calculation is based come directly from the customer. Only in this way can the seller create trust. In the end, the customer decides not only for the product but for the overall performance presented by the salesperson.

5. Challenger Selling: Luring the customer out of the r serve

The challenger selling method is the most modern and most popular sales strategy among salespeople at the moment. This is because the method developed by CEB Global is based on scientifically collected data from over 1000 sales managers from various industries and is essentially based on the Solution Selling Method, which is already highly regarded among sales people. Unlike Solution Selling, however, the "Challenger" places less emphasis on reaching a consensus than the Solution Seller. With Challenger Selling, the seller is more interested in opening up a new business approach for the potential customer. He challenges the customer's business model, so to speak. The challenger sale focuses on effective questioning on how the customer is currently doing business today and then understanding the challenges and pains that come along with it. Once that is complete the sales person then proposes an applicable alternative that will enhance and add

additional value to the existing methodology. This strategy is built around creating a moment where you challenge the customer's preconceived notions and truly teach them something new.

This method is particularly successful when the own product offers innovative advantages that were simply not possible up to now. Examples are technologies such as mobile telephones, the Internet and artificial intelligence. If the sales employee succeeds in creating an aha effect with the customer without questioning the customer's best practices too much, he has already taken a big step towards signing a contract. The business partner has learnt something new and already knows the necessary tool to apply what he has learnt - your product.

CHAPTER 4

HUMAN RESOURCE MANAGEMENT

Human resource management is the management of people in organizations from a macro perspective i.e., managing people in the form of a collective relationship between management and employees. This approach focuses on the objectives and outcomes of the HRM function. What this means is that the HR function in contemporary organizations is concerned with the notions of people enabling, people development and a focus on making the "employment relationship" fulfilling for both the management and employees. It is designed to maximize employee performance in service of an employer's strategic objectives. Human Resource Management is the process of managing people in organizations in a structured and thorough manner. This covers the fields of staffing (hiring people), retention of people, pay and perks setting and management, performance management, change management and taking care of exits from the company to round off the activities. This is the traditional definition of HRM which leads some experts to define it as a modern version of the Personnel Management function that was used earlier.

Key Functions of Human Resources

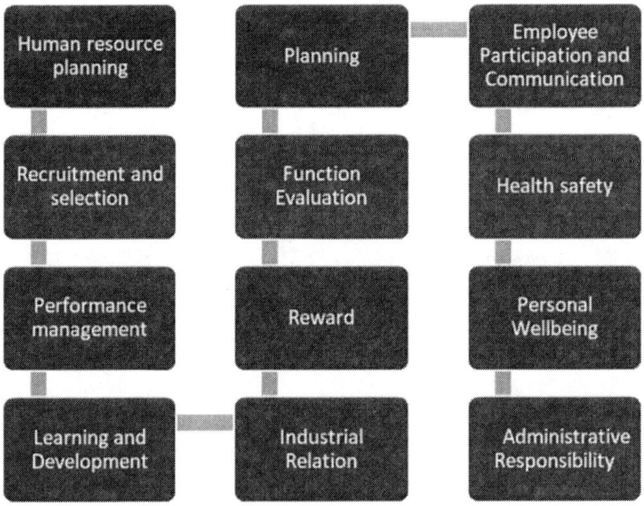

1. Human resource planning

The first HR function is all about knowing the future needs of the organization. What kind of people does the organization need, and how many? Knowing this will shape recruitment, selection, performance management, learning and development, and all other human resources functions. Human resources planning is similar to workforce planning. Both focus on where the organization is today and what it needs to be successful in the future.

2. Recruitment and selection

The second HR function involves attracting people to work for the organization and selecting the best candidates. Attracting people usually starts with an employee brand. Being an attractive employer has plenty of advantages - just as it is the other way around. A good example of the latter is the tobacco industry which struggles to attract talent due to its tainted reputation. With a strong employer brand and the right sourcing strategies, you're already halfway there. Once candidates apply, the selection process is an HR instrument to pick the best qualified and highest-

potential candidates. Technological developments in recruitment have gone very fast and as a result, there are different types of recruitment tools for each part of your recruitment funnel.

3. Performance management

Performance management is essential in ensuring that workers stay productive and engaged. Good performance management involves good leadership, clear goal-setting, and open feedback. Performance management tools include the (bi)annual performance review, in which the employee is reviewed by his/her manager. It also includes 360-degree feedback tools in which peers, managers, subordinates, and sometimes even customers review the employee's performance. These kinds of tools can be very helpful in providing feedback. Performance management is also an instrument to close the gap between the workforce you have today and the one you want to have tomorrow. One of the best ways to build your future workforce is through learning and development (L&D).

4. Learning and development

Enabling employees to develop the skills they need for the future is an essential responsibility for HR. This is also related to the first HR function we listed, in which HR bridges the gap between the workforce today and the workforce needed in the near future.

5. Career planning

The fifth function of Human Resource Management is career planning, guidance, and development for employees, together also referred to as career pathing.

6. Function evaluation

As a business and society changes, so too must an efficient HR function. Function evaluation is a technical aspect of HR. By evaluating the HR function, the department ensures that the company is successful at both a strategic level and with service delivery and support. The company needs to deliver the level of services required,

whilst operating strategically. Practically, function evaluation involves comparing various parts of the overall HR operation. This can include the quality, and availability of workers, job location, working times, the economic situation, job responsibilities, and how much value a job adds to your organization. The idea behind function evaluation is that similar jobs should be rewarded similarly.

There are different ways of internally ranking functions.

- Ranking method: a method in which subject matter experts rank functions in terms of how much they contribute to the organization as a whole. Functions are paired and raters have to decide which one is more valuable. This is done with all functions and based on the outcome, a ranking is established.
- Classification method: jobs can also be classified in different categories using classification methods. In this case, jobs are categorized and then ranked within these categories to come up with a ranking. Categorizations can include education, experience, the degree of specialized skills needed to do the job, the degree to which these skills are in-demand, and so on.
- Points method: jobs are categorized according to the factors the organization believes contribute most to its success. Points are then awarded to each category for every job. These categories can include key competencies, like problem-solving, technical knowledge, communication and influencing skills, innovative capability, business acumen, and so on. These competencies will differ per organization
- Personal method: in this method, the job itself is not evaluated but the person doing the job is. Here, employees are rewarded based on their skills and competencies.

7. Rewards

Rewarding employees for their work is a function that is impossible to miss. Compensation and benefits are integral to attracting the right kind of candidate for the role, and company.

These will vary across different fields, countries, and cultures. In some countries, such as the USA, health insurance is often part of a job offer. However, in countries such as the UK, where a public health system provides most healthcare, to most people, this is not the case. Yet the total rewards framework shows that rewards are more than just money. They can also be relational and psychological outcomes. Rewards include salary but also growth and career opportunities, status, recognition, a good organizational culture, and a satisfying work-life balance. For example, fantastic colleagues and meaningful work are also rewarding to employees. The monetary reward of the job consists of financial rewards and other (secondary) benefits.

AIHR-Elements-of-Total-Rewards

The Employee Value Proposition (EVP) sums up all these aspects. The EVP of your company is distinct from the external image and brand. It is the image a company reflects to its employees. Rewards are thus much more than just financial. Here is a non-exhaustive overview of total rewards:

Base salary

Performance-based-pay

Bonuses

Social environment

Job security

Status

Alternating work

Autonomy

Growth opportunities

Feedback

Formal and informal development opportunities

Functions 1 to 7 all fall within the scope of what's called talent management; they aim to attract, develop, motivate and retain (high-performing) employees.

8. Industrial relations

Another function of HR is maintaining and cultivating relationships with labour unions and other collectives, and their members.

Unionization is still prevalent in Europe, although it is declining overall. In 2018, 92% of employees in Iceland were a member of a union and 67% of employees in Denmark. However, in the UK and Estonia, only 23% and 4% of employees, respectively, were. In the USA trade union membership is low, with 10% of employees being members in 2018. Maintaining good relations with unions will help to spot and resolve potential conflicts quickly and will also be beneficial in more difficult economic times when layoffs or other actions are required.

9. Employee participation and communication

According to Dave Ulrich, one of the key roles of HR is to be a credible activist for the employees. Employees need to be informed and heard on different topics that are relevant to them. Communication relates to spreading information relevant to employees. Being a People's Advocate is one of five elements of the T-shaped HR professional, a new competency framework we developed for the future of the HR workforce. People Advocacy includes culture building, people practices, workplace champion, and communication expert.

10. Health and safety

HR plays an important role in creating and implementing health and safety regulations. Making these regulations part of the company culture is one of the main functions of HR. A famous example is the oil company Shell where it is forbidden to walk the

stairs without holding the railing - also in the company's HQ. This is part of Shell's 'Goal Zero', which stands for zero accidents. Although holding the railing is much more important on an oil platform, safety is such a big part of the company culture that safety roles are applied everywhere.

11. Personal wellbeing

HR has the function of assisting and taking care of employees when they run into personal problems. Personal wellbeing is about supporting employees when things don't go as planned. Problems in the workplace and outside can negatively impact employee performance, engagement, and productivity. This, in turn, harms a company's bottom line.

Good personal well-being led by your HR department must work at the level of one-on-one communication with employees, and communication across teams, and companies. For example, a company may offer an employee assistance program by which anyone with mental health issues, can access counselling. On an organization-wide level, the company could hold a mental health awareness day.

12. Administrative responsibilities

The final function of HR is its administrative responsibility. These include personnel procedures and Human Resource Information Systems. Personnel procedures involve the handling of promotions, relocations, discipline, performance improvement, illness, regulations, cultural and racial diversity, unwanted intimacies, bullying, and so on. For each of these situations, policies and procedures need to be developed and followed to successfully comply with the requests, or overcome these challenges.

Human Resource Information Systems (HRIS) store employee data. These systems need to be purchased, implemented and managed so the data can be used for better decision-making.

Role of Human Resource Management (HRM) in Leadership Development

Leadership Development in Successful Companies

The previous articles have discussed how the HRM function is now seen as a critical and crucial component of the organizational support functions. In particular, we have analysed how effective people management goes a long way in ensuring better economic performance. Among the components of people, management that the HRM function does is the aspect related to leadership development.

Research into the HRM practices of successful companies has shown that these companies significantly outperform their peers in terms of economic profitability by following the leadership development practices discussed in this article. By successful companies, we mean those companies on the Fortune 100 list that have managed to retain their position in the firms for over a decade. To put this in perspective, it needs to be remembered that many companies that were in the Fortune 100 list for a few years failed to retain their positions in subsequent years and hence, the fact that these companies have managed to stay in the hunt means that they have outperformed their peers and competitors.

The Components of Leadership Development

The leadership development programs in these companies follow the philosophy of grounding them in value, the expected contributions from the leaders are defined, and the organizational culture is geared towards inspiring leaders. Next, the performance management system in these companies is tied to the company's business strategy and it includes talent development activities and leadership objectives that are articulated clearly and succinctly. In other words, promotions are based on individual performance as well as people development activities and these, in turn, are linked to the business strategy and objectives.

These companies also have a leadership pipeline, which means that the leadership development is embedded in their strategic workforce planning which is comprehensive, and longer term oriented. These companies also ensure that they divide their workforce into job families and the potential leaders are identified and groomed for higher roles and responsibilities. In many of these companies, it is common to find lists of potential leaders known as high potentials who are earmarked for fast track career progression based on the organizational assessment of the skills and capabilities of these leaders. Further, the recruitment and training of new employees are based on longer-term analysis of demand and supply patterns, which ensure that a newer generation of leaders are hired into the company to replace those who have made it to the higher levels.

Collaboration between the HRM Function and Senior Management

The HRM functions in these companies work on a collaborative model with their potential leaders which means that the job of people development is not left to the HRM function or the leaders alone. Instead, the potential leaders are identified and then their performance is linked to the enabling

and empowerment of others to move up the chain. In other words, the ability to spot talent and identify leaders for the future is done by both the HRM function and the senior management who work in tandem in this effort.

Research into these successful companies has shown that the people management in these companies is world-class and the contributing factor that differentiates these companies from others is that the HRM function plays a critical role throughout the employee lifecycle and not at the recruitment and training phase alone. The other factor is that the leaders in these companies are expected to have skill sets that match the need for adapting to the challenges of the 21st-century business landscape. In other words, these companies groom the leaders of the future right from the middle management level.

Closing Thoughts

Finally, leadership is a combination of natural abilities and the organizational nurturing of the employees with those skills. Hence, this interplay between nature and nurture is what determines the success or otherwise of the HRM function and the senior management efforts to develop leadership in these companies.

Hiring Strategies followed by Organizations

People are the lifeblood of any organization. Whether the organization is in the traditional sectors like manufacturing or it is a "new economy" based one like IT and ITES, it needs to be staffed with people of calibres and mettle. Hence, the kind of people that an organization hires is critical to the success of the organization. In this respect, the hiring strategies followed by organizations take on prominence in the competitive business environment of the 21st-century.

Hiring can take place in many ways and at many levels. It can be for entry-level positions or "lateral" hiring where people with experience are taken on board. Further, hiring people can be based on competitive exams (entry-level) and the personal

approach favoured by HR managers for senior-level positions. In recent times, hiring for the entry-level has taken on an entirely new dimension with the campus recruitment procedures that rely on getting the best talent available from the campuses for companies wishing to hire for entry-level positions. The other way of hiring is through selective approach where the Staffing department entrusts the placement consultants with the task of identifying potential employees by picking "profiles" from employee databases and the consultants' own database as well.

As outlined above, the different hiring strategies are for different levels in the organization. The most niche hiring takes place at senior levels where the essence is discreetness and hence dedicated consultants or HR professionals approach people at higher levels on a one-one basis.

Whatever be the hiring strategy deployed, the essential components of the process remain more or less the same. These include choosing from the available candidates, taking a decision as to the pay and perks, making an offer and finally, getting them "on board". The hiring process ranges from as less a month or so to draw out affairs for niche placement. The strategic imperatives that underpin hiring depend on the ability of the organization to effectively leverage its reputation, flexibility in the roles that are available, availability of skilled resources and finally, the package that the organization is willing to offer.

Most debates in organizations on the hiring process hinge on the length of time it takes to hire a person for a particular role and the package that the organization is willing to offer. The term "fitment" is often used as HR jargon which is all about whether a particular person is suitable for the role that is being filled and how well he or she "fits" the job profile. One of the reasons for attrition in organizations is the fact that many employees join them with a set of assumptions about their role only to have their hopes dashed in reality. Hence, in recent times, industry experts have focused on this aspect of ensuring that people are hired only if they are the right fit.

In conclusion, hiring people is a key component of a company's internal strategy and hence something that needs detailed attention and focus. We have touched upon the hiring strategies and the overview of the process. In subsequent articles, we would explore the topic further.

Retention Strategies - Definition and its Components

Any employee retention strategy would necessarily include a plan for redressing employee grievances and ways and means to address employee issues. This would mean that the employees would be enabled to take their issues regarding pay, their work, their role etc. to the HR manager for each division and expect to get a fair hearing in the process. There should be a plan where the HR manager in conjunction with the manager of the employee who has raised the issue works towards resolving the issue.

Components of a Retention Strategy

Taking each of these strategies in turn, job rotation is the practice of moving the employees around divisions and within divisions with a clear emphasis on making sure that they operate in domains other than the ones assigned to them initially. This would mean that the employees get trained on competencies beyond that of their assigned plant and this would lead to greater motivation to pick up additional skills and motivate them to perform better. The importance of grievance redressal and mitigation cannot be emphasised more. This is the most critical and crucial component of the HRM plan as research has shown that an employee with pending issues awaiting resolution is twice more likely to quit the company than the other employees. Hence, all efforts must be made to redress the grievances of the employees.

Grievance Redressal

An effective retention strategy would focus on preventing as well as addressing grievances. Though it is not the contention

that all grievances can be prevented, they can be "pre-empted" by actively listening to the employees from time to time. This strategy of "listening" to the employees would revolve around a concept of "one-one" meetings between the employees and the manager and employees and the HR representative for the unit or division. The idea of the regular "one-one" meetings would be to identify potential causes of friction among the employees and any issues they may have vis-à-vis their job and benefits. These issues need to be brought out into the open before they become contentious resulting in the employee feeling frustrated and quitting the job. Hence, all efforts must be made to identify sources of employee dissatisfaction and "hygiene factors" that must be taken care of for the proper functioning of the employees.

Ways to Mitigate Job Dissatisfaction

Management theorists often emphasise the fact that one of the reasons for low employee morale in organizations is the fact that the employees and often feel alienated and cut off from the larger purpose. The contention is that the employees feel themselves to be part of an impersonal setup and perceive themselves to be unable to make a difference to the whole unit. Hence, there is a need to involve the employees in the larger picture and provide them with perspective on the bigger picture. In engineering units with assembly line manufacturing, the engineer is often responsible for his or her part of the chain and is not in a position to relate to the bigger picture. Hence, there should be effective strategies like job rotation, interaction with other units, timely promotions and cross functional teams wherein the engineers would feel themselves to be contributing to the larger goal of the company.

Staffing Role of the HR Manager: Strategic Workforce Planning

Staffing and Recruiting during the Boom Years

One of the key areas that the HRM unit works with is the staffing function. Hiring and onboarding of employees remain a critical activity that many HR managers are yet to master. This

is mainly because of the unevenness of the demand and supply in the market for talent. For instance, during the heady years of the IT boom in the early years of the last decade, it was common for many division heads and line managers to walk into the HR manager's office and give him or her target of employees to be recruited over the next three months in the quarter.

In the US, the situation was that many HR managers were asked to take in as many H1B or temporary workers to the country on board to meet the critical shortage in staff. In Asia, because of this very reason where many techies had headed to the US and Europe, hiring became a challenge for even the most seasoned HR professionals. The implications for the HR manager are many as his or her appraisal depends on a number of targets including how many they have recruited over the last quarter or the year.

Strategies to Deal with Shortage of Talent during the Boom Years

The way to deal with such a situation was to ensure that the number of people being taken in was based on current and future demand scenarios and to identify gaps and surpluses in key skill sets. For instance, in the US, the shortage of those with Java skills was so huge that anyone with an elementary knowledge of the skill was immediately taken into the companies. This meant that the HR unit was simply filling up positions without any strategic planning. Hence, many organizations realized that hiring people without the requisite skills just to fill up positions would do more harm than good to the companies and hence, a conscious decision was taken by the HR managers in conjunction with the line managers to have forecasts of how many employees they would need over a quarter. The point here is that the constant bickering between the HR managers and the line managers took a toll on organizational efficiency and hence, this compromise was arrived at wherein the demand for specific skill sets had to be forecasted by the line managers and the HR managers would then deal with hiring accordingly.

The third aspect of the staffing and hiring activity is that many HR managers during the boom years advised the line managers to find employees from other divisions who wanted a change in their job profiles and roles. This internal filling up of positions by inter-division and intra-company movement was effective in many companies like Fidelity. Further, overtime by key resources and hiring temporary workers were the norm in many companies. Of course, the overtime work was adequately compensated and employees who were doing so were given additional benefits.

Staffing Strategies during the Ongoing Recession

With the boom years over, the HR managers in recent years are breathing easy as they no longer have to run around trying to meet recruitment targets. Of course, the current challenge before the HR managers is to manage the downturn and smoothen the downsizing underway in many organizations. To ensure these objectives in these economically harsh times, HR managers are resorting to passive measures as the first line of action wherein they indicate to the employees that they are on PIP or Performance Improvement Plans and this usually results in natural attrition. Next, instead of downsizing, the HR managers are reducing recruitment so that they do not have to fire employees and instead, these employees can be accommodated elsewhere in the organization. These are some of the aspects of strategic workplace planning within the hiring and staffing activity that some respected companies follow.

CHAPTER 5

Strategic Management

Strategic management is the process of setting goals, procedures, and objectives in order to make a company or organization more competitive. Typically, strategic management looks at effectively deploying staff and resources to achieve these goals. Often, strategic management includes strategy evaluation, internal organization analysis, and strategy execution throughout the company. Strategic management is the ongoing planning, monitoring, analysis and assessment of all necessities an organization needs to meet its goals and objectives. Changes in business environments will require organizations to constantly assess their strategies for success. The strategic management process helps organizations take stock of their present situation, chalk out strategies, deploy them and analyse the effectiveness of the implemented management strategies. Strategic management strategies consist of five basic strategies and can differ in implementation depending on the surrounding environment. Strategic management applies both to on-premise and mobile platforms.

Strategic management process

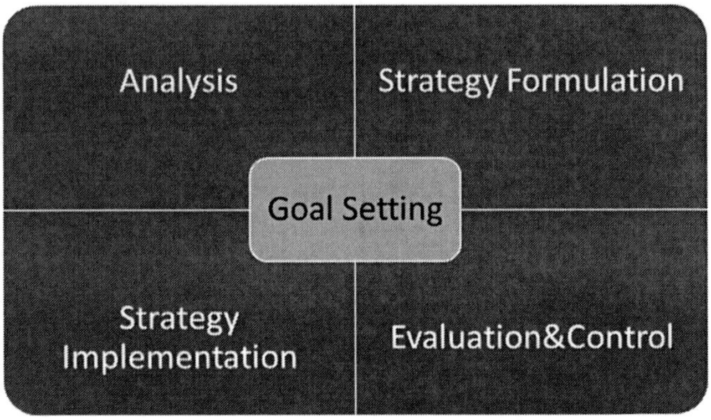

The 5 stages of the strategic management process

The strategic management process is more than a set of rules to follow. It is a philosophical approach to business. Top management must think strategically first, then apply that thinking to a process. The process is best implemented when everyone in the business understands the strategy.

1. Goal setting

How to set business goals and strategies. The purpose of setting goals is to clarify the business vision. This stage consists of identifying three facets: First, define the short- and long-term objectives. Second, identify the process of how to achieve the objectives. Finally, personalize the process according to our staff, give each member a task with which they can be successful. During this process, check that the objectives are detailed, realistic, and coincide with the values of your business vision. Typically, the final step at this stage is to make these goals and objectives known to all staff.

2. Analysis

The analysis is a key stage because the information obtained in this stage will configure the following two stages. At this stage, collect relevant information and data to achieve your vision. The

focus of strategic analysis should be to understand the business needs as a sustainable entity, with strategic and identify initiatives that will help the business to grow. Examine any external or internal problems that may affect your goals and objectives. Be sure to identify the strengths and weaknesses of your organization, as well as the threats and opportunities that may arise along the way.

3. Strategy formulation

The first step in forming a strategy is to review the information obtained from the analysis. Determine what resources the business currently has that can help achieve defined goals and objectives. Identify any area from which external resources should be sought. The problems facing the company must be prioritized for its importance to be successful. Once prioritized, begin formulating the strategy.

4. Strategy implementation

The successful implementation of the strategy is essential for the success of the company. If the overall strategy does not work with the current business structure, a new structure must be installed at the beginning of this stage. Everyone within the organization must be clear about their responsibilities and duties, and how this fit in with the overall goal. In addition, all resources or funds for the company must be guaranteed at this time. Once financing is in place and employees are ready, execute the plan.

5. Evaluation and control

Any successful evaluation of the strategy begins with the definition of the parameters to be measured. These parameters should reflect the goals established in Stage 1. Determine your progress by measuring actual results versus the plan. Monitoring internal and external problems will also allow you to react to any substantial change in your business environment. If you determine that the strategy is not moving the company toward its goal, take corrective action. If those actions are not successful,

repeat the strategic management process. Because internal and external issues are constantly evolving, all data obtained at this stage should be kept to help with any future strategy.

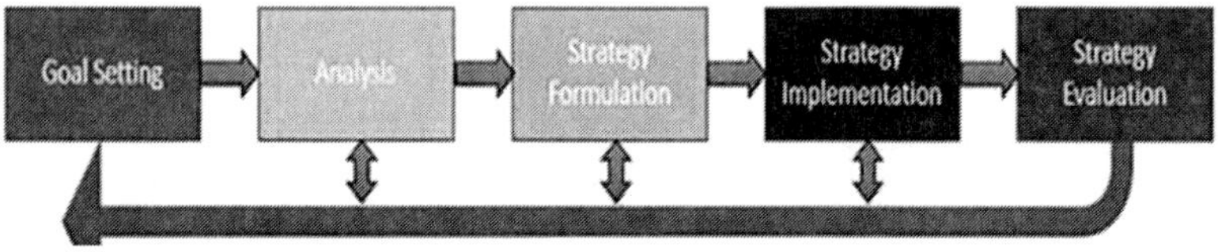

4 STEPS TO EFFECTIVELY IMPLEMENT STRATEGIC MANAGEMENT

There are several stages in the strategic management process. While the outcome will look different from business to business, there are simple chronological steps that organisations can follow to put strategies into practice.

Step 1: Strategic intent - Successful execution of strategic management starts with strategic intent – that's defining the organisational objectives and using them as a benchmark to measure performance and progress. An organisation's vision and direction should be specific, actionable and measurable, rather than broad. This is the point where companies outline their future business focus – whether that's profitability, shareholder wealth, or market leadership.

Step 2: Strategy formulation - The next stage involves formulating the strategy and this requires a company health check through a SWOT analysis. It's where companies forensically examine themselves, looking at the environment they operate in, both internally and externally. This strategic analysis focuses on company strengths, weaknesses, opportunities and threats. Through this process, an organisation is able to determine what it does better than its competition, what it needs to improve on, and what advantages its competitors have. This will then help them develop ideas on how to outcompete rivals and respond

to changing market conditions. This is also the stage when companies determine where they are and where they want to be. Once an assessment is made, it's time to implement the strategy.

Step 3: Strategy implementation - An organisational blueprint is a good start to strategic management, but it must be put into action. To ensure a company's survival, growth and expansion, strategies must be put into practice. It's estimated that more than 60% of the strategies are not successfully implemented. Success requires:

Developing structures and systems,

Allocating resources,

Overseeing change management,

Instigating risk management strategies,

Developing decision-making processes,

Developing project management capabilities,

Strengthening competitive capabilities,

Communicating strategy,

Managing human resources by aligning individual roles with performance objectives; and

Rewarding performance.

Execution of strategic plans allows organisations to explore new opportunities and brings into line all aspects of a company—people, strategy and operations.

Step 4: Strategy evaluation - The final stage of strategic management is to analyse and assess the results achieved through the strategic process. By measuring the performance of an organisational strategy, companies can decide whether to stay on course or make adjustments to correct actions to adapt to changing market conditions. This is an ongoing process that gives organisations the opportunity to review performance metrics and put interventions in place if necessary.

5 BENEFITS OF STRATEGIC PLANNING

1. Creates a sense of direction

A strategic plan helps to create a sense of purpose and to define the direction in which an organisation must travel, and aids in establishing realistic objectives and goals that are in line with the vision and mission charted out for it. It also creates the necessary foundation and boundaries to determine resource allocation and efficient decision-making in the following areas (e.g. budget allocation, hiring decisions, operational processes, marketing strategy etc.

2. Increase operational efficiency

With a clear plan and direction in place, resources could be channelled and monitored more effectively to ensure that effectiveness is enhanced and wastage is reduced. Effective goals and KPIs could be set and measured to determine the progress and growth of the organisation.

3. Increase market share and profitability

By crafting and adopting a dedicated strategic plan, organisations can get valuable insights into market trends, consumer segments, and buying behaviour/patterns. With a well-planned and targeted approach, a clear strategic intent could be channelled into sales and marketing efforts, leading to a higher possibility of increasing profitability and market share.

4. Increase durability and sustainability

Businesses are constantly adapting to change, especially in a digitally-led economy. The purpose of strategic planning is to flag out potential internal/external shocks and prepare the business to be more effective in adapting. With industry trends and consumer demands constantly changing, organisations that lack a strong foundation, focus and foresight will have difficulties riding the next wave.

5. Being proactive instead of reactive

The current dynamic business environment requires every business to be equipped with a good strategic plan. Strategic planning enables your business to stay ahead of the curve and be on top of the competition. It will also enable your business to find and benefit from potential opportunities present in the market.

The Office of Strategy Management

An office of strategy management, or OSM, is intended to close that gap. It is typically a new unit at the corporate level of an organization, overseeing all strategy-related activities–from formulation to execution.

Key Tasks of Strategy Office

Strategic work, however, varies significantly depending on the objectives, sector and management culture of the company. Strategy is often interpreted in many ways, and its significance to interest groups depends on the viewpoint.

The key is to carry out the right operations at exactly the right time. Successfulness of decision making, and eliciting the participation of the employees are critical points that always concern companies.

Strategy office is a scouting post

Observing the business environment is a key aspect of strategizing. According to studies, 65% of a company's success is based on its ability to adapt to changes in the business environment and utilise the subsequently arising business opportunities. While a strategy office is a fairly new concept and method in Finland, it has garnered plenty of interest. Strategy office facilitates the organisation of, e.g., the following operations:

Communicating strategic work to employees and other key interest groups

Measuring and evaluating strategy (e.g. KGI, strategic coherence analysis, strategic project, application and service portfolio analyses, value gap analyses)

Planning and management of the strategy process

Creating strategic partnerships

Scenario work

In-house support for management

Strategic resource allocation

Strategic risk management (current issues, e.g., geopolitical matters and market risks)

It is good practice to establish who the strategy office reports to, and how the organisation can provide information required by the strategy office.

Why is Strategic Management Necessary?

Strategic management helps the person in charge of decision-making get secured with management tools or to expect the changes by guiding the organizational activities on the right

path. In addition, strategic management's practice lessens the operational risk by assisting the enterprise to innovate in time and take action beforehand. The following are why strategic management is vital in the organization.

Helps To Anticipate the Changes

As discussed above, strategic management requires the manager to study the company's future and the market. Researching the future continuously. The managers can anticipate the change. When done effectively, strategic management can lead the organization to proact to a change or even bring around the change in the market. Strategic management lets the companies make decisions based on detailed forecasts and not impulsive reactions. It enables the firm to take measures at a primitive stage of a new trend and reckon the lead time for efficient management.

Clarity In Objectives and Direction

Strategic management renders a strong inducement for the employees and management to attain company objectives. Strategic management also guarantees that the top executives have a united opinion on strategic problems.

Increases Employee Efficiency

The employees at all levels are included in the strategic management process. As a result, the employees feel more engaged and motivated to work. Necessary training is provided to the employees, and the inter-process of strategy implementation is done through the employees. This increases the efficiency of the employees. With a strategic workflow the performance management of the organizations is benefited. When the employees feel they are a part of the organization's more astonishing view and are considered necessary to fulfill the organizational goals, they will be willing to give their best to the company.

Rises Profitability

The business unit's profitability depends upon the maximum utilization of the available resources. Therefore, the managers can make full use of financial resources and use maximum labor capacity to increase the unit's productivity and profitability with the help of strategic management.

Reduces Expenses

Strategic management helps the organization to reduce its expenses on unnecessary investments. For example, the fixed capital of any company is the amount invested in its fixed assets. With the help of strategic management, the managers may decide whether it would be profitable to invest in these fixed assets or rent them to decrease the fixed capital investment.

Fills The Organizational Gap

An organizational gap is an activity from departmental activities not assigned to any employee. If such allotment is left out mistakenly, no employee can be held responsible for it. Because of the constant interaction and communication undertaken within the strategic management process, every employee receives equal work. Due to this reason, organizational gaps that delay the business's goal-achieving capability can be avoided entirely. With strategic management, this hurdle is conquered.

Interesting Facts to Know About Strategic Management

More than 97% of employers feel that strategy implementation is challenging than strategy formulation.

67% of the employers have stated that their organizations successfully craft the best strategies. However, only about 45%-47% of them succeed in their implementation.

More than 65% of the formulated strategies fail due to a lack of proper implementation.

While 18% of the employers say that hiring candidates with the necessary skills to drive the strategy's implementation is a high priority, 11% of the employers are developing and enhancing such skills in the already existing employees.

More than 60% of the companies that have established a formal process to manage the strategic decisions have out-performed their competitors.

Only about 20% of the companies review their strategic decision's execution monthly.

About 4% of the strategic management's potential is lost due to the lack of defined accountabilities.

Strategy Evaluation Process and its Significance

Strategy Evaluation is as significant as strategy formulation because it throws light on the efficiency and effectiveness of the comprehensive plans in achieving the desired results. The managers can also assess the appropriateness of the current strategy in today's dynamic world with socio-economic, political and technological innovations. Strategic Evaluation is the final phase of strategic management.

The significance of strategy evaluation lies in its capacity to co-ordinate the task performed by managers, groups, departments etc, through control of performance. Strategic Evaluation is significant because of various factors such as - developing inputs for new strategic planning, the urge for feedback, appraisal and reward, development of the strategic management process, judging the validity of strategic choice etc.

The process of Strategy Evaluation consists of following steps:-

1. Fixing benchmark of performance - While fixing the benchmark, strategists encounter questions such as - what benchmarks to set, how to set them and how to express them. In order to determine the benchmark performance

to be set, it is essential to discover the special requirements for performing the main task. The performance indicator that best identify and express the special requirements might then be determined to be used for evaluation. The organization can use both quantitative and qualitative criteria for comprehensive assessment of performance. Quantitative criteria includes determination of net profit, ROI, earning per share, cost of production, rate of employee turnover etc. Among the Qualitative factors are subjective evaluation of factors such as - skills and competencies, risk taking potential, flexibility etc.

2. Measurement of performance - The standard performance is a bench mark with which the actual performance is to be compared. The reporting and communication system help in measuring the performance. If appropriate means are available for measuring the performance and if the standards are set in the right manner, strategy evaluation becomes easier. But various factors such as managers contribution are difficult to measure. Similarly divisional performance is sometimes difficult to measure as compared to individual performance. Thus, variable objectives must be created against which measurement of performance can be done. The measurement must be done at right time else evaluation will not meet its purpose. For measuring the performance, financial statements like - balance sheet, profit and loss account must be prepared on an annual basis.

3. Analysing Variance - While measuring the actual performance and comparing it with standard performance there may be variances which must be analysed. The strategists must mention the degree of tolerance limits between which the variance between actual and standard performance may be accepted. The positive deviation indicates a better performance but it is quite unusual exceeding the target

always. The negative deviation is an issue of concern because it indicates a shortfall in performance. Thus in this case the strategists must discover the causes of deviation and must take corrective action to overcome it.

4. Taking Corrective Action - Once the deviation in performance is identified, it is essential to plan for a corrective action. If the performance is consistently less than the desired performance, the strategists must carry a detailed analysis of the factors responsible for such performance. If the strategists discover that the organizational potential does not match with the performance requirements, then the standards must be lowered. Another rare and drastic corrective action is reformulating the strategy which requires going back to the process of strategic management, reframing of plans according to new resource allocation trend and consequent means going to the beginning point of strategic management process.

Components of a Strategy Statement

The strategy statement of a firm sets the firm's long-term strategic direction and broad policy directions. It gives the firm a clear sense of direction and a blueprint for the firm's activities for the upcoming years. The main constituents of a strategic statement are as follows:

Strategic Intent

An organization's strategic intent is the purpose that it exists and why it will continue to exist, providing it maintains a competitive advantage. Strategic intent gives a picture about what an organization must get into immediately in order to achieve the company's vision. It motivates the people. It clarifies the vision of the vision of the company.

Strategic intent helps management to emphasize and concentrate on the priorities. Strategic intent is, nothing but, the influencing of an organization's resource potential and core

competencies to achieve what at first may seem to be unachievable goals in the competitive environment. A well-expressed strategic intent should guide/steer the development of strategic intent or the setting of goals and objectives that require that all of organization's competencies be controlled to maximum value.

Strategic intent includes directing organization's attention on the need of winning; inspiring people by telling them that the targets are valuable; encouraging individual and team participation as well as contribution, and utilizing intent to direct the allocation of resources.

Strategic intent differs from strategic fit in way that while strategic fit deals with harmonizing available resources and potentials to the external environment, strategic intent emphasizes building new resources and potentials so as to create and exploit future opportunities.

Mission Statement

Mission statement is the statement of the role by which an organization intends to serve it's stakeholders. It describes why an organization is operating and thus provides a framework within which strategies are formulated. It describes what the organization does (i.e., present capabilities), who all it serves (i.e., stakeholders) and what makes an organization unique (i.e., reason for existence).

A mission statement differentiates an organization from others by explaining its broad scope of activities, its products, and the technologies it uses to achieve its goals and objectives. It talks about an organization's present (i.e., "about where we are"). For instance, Microsoft's mission is to help people and businesses throughout the world to realize their full potential. Wal-Mart's mission is "To give ordinary folk the chance to buy the same thing as rich people." Mission statements always exist at the top level of an organization, but may also be made for various organizational levels. The Chief executive plays a significant role in the formulation of mission

statement. Once the mission statement is formulated, it serves the organization in long run, but it may become ambiguous with organizational growth and innovations.

In today's dynamic and competitive environment, mission may need to be redefined. However, care must be taken that the redefined mission statement should have original fundamentals/ components. Mission statement has three main components-a statement of mission or vision of the company, a statement of the core values that shape the acts and behaviour of the employees, and a statement of the goals and objectives.

Features of a Mission

- Mission must be feasible and attainable. It should be possible to achieve it.
- Mission should be clear enough so that any action can be taken.
- It should be inspiring for the management, staff and society at large.
- It should be precise enough, i.e., it should be neither too broad nor too narrow.
- It should be unique and distinctive to leave an impact in everyone's mind.
- It should be analytical., it should analyse the key components of the strategy.
- It should be credible, i.e., all stakeholders should be able to believe it.

Vision

A vision statement identifies where the organization wants or intends to be in future or where it should be to best meet the needs of the stakeholders. It describes dreams and aspirations for the future. For instance, Microsoft's vision is "to empower people through great software, any time, any place, or any device." Wal-Mart's vision is to become the worldwide leader in retailing.

A vision is the potential to view things ahead of themselves. It answers the question "where we want to be". It gives us a reminder about what we attempt to develop. A vision statement is for the organization and its members, unlike the mission statement which is for the customers/clients. It contributes to effective decision making as well as effective business planning. It incorporates a shared understanding of the nature and aim of the organization and utilizes this understanding to direct and guide the organization towards a better purpose. It describes that on achieving the mission, how the organizational future would appear to be.

An effective vision statement must have following features:-

- It must be unambiguous.
- It must be clear.
- It must harmonize with organization's culture and values.
- The dreams and aspirations must be rational/realistic.
- Vision statements should be shorter so that they are easier to memorize.

In order to realize the vision, it must be deeply instilled in the organization, is owned and shared by everyone involved in the organization.

Goals and Objectives

A goal is a desired future state or objective that an organization tries to achieve. Goals specify in particular what must be done if an organization is to attain mission or vision. Goals make mission more prominent and concrete. They co-ordinate and integrate various functional and departmental areas in an organization. Well-made goals have following features:

- These are precise and measurable.
- These look after critical and significant issues.
- These are realistic and challenging.

- These must be achieved within a specific time frame.
- These include both financial as well as non-financial components.

Objectives are defined as goals that organization wants to achieve over a period of time. These are the foundation of planning. Policies are developed in an organization so as to achieve these objectives. Formulation of objectives is the task of top-level management. Effective objectives have following features:-

- These are not single for an organization, but multiple.
- Objectives should be both short-term as well as long-term.
- Objectives must respond and react to changes in environment, i.e., they must be flexible.
- These must be feasible, realistic and operational.

CHAPTER 6

Production Management

Production management, also called operations management, planning and control of industrial processes to ensure that they move smoothly at the required level. Techniques of production management are employed in service as well as in manufacturing industries. Operations management is an area of management concerned with designing and controlling the process of production and redesigning business operations in the production of goods or services. It is a responsibility similar in level and scope to other specialties such as marketing or human resource and financial management. In manufacturing operations, production management includes responsibility for product and process design, planning and control issues involving capacity and quality, and organization and supervision of the workforce.

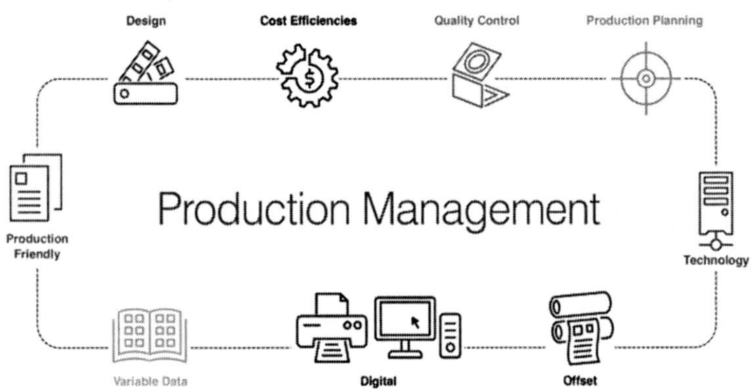

Five Types of Production Planning

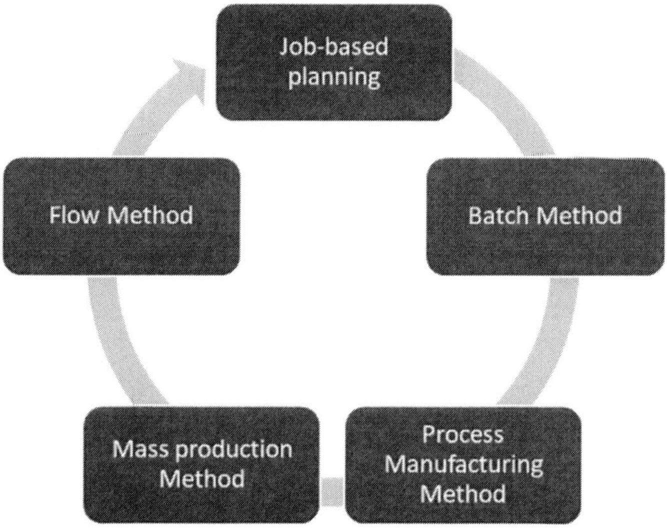

1. Job-Based Planning

Job-Based or Project-Based production focuses on manufacturing a single product and is either handled by a single worker or by a group of people. The type of jobs that fall under this type of production planning can be on a small scale, such as creating a customized piece of jewelry. Larger, more complex production projects, such as building customized houses, also fall into this category.

Production planning for small-scale jobs that require very little specialized equipment is relatively easy to execute. This allows products to be made according to their customer's requests and can usually be included at any time during the production process without altering its progress.

2. Batch Method

Batch production is used when items are produced in groups, rather than individually or through continuous production. For example, cookies are produced in batches which means that each production step occurs at the same time on the batch

of cookies. You will start by measuring the ingredients for the entire batch, then mix them together, and finally bake them together so that the entire production process for the batch of cookies starts and ends at the same time.

The challenge that can occur when using Batch Production planning is accounting for the constraints at each operation step to ensure that you maximize your resource capacity without going over the maximum limit allowed. For example, if your dough mixer can fit a batch of 100 cookies, but you can only bake 300 at a time, you may encounter bottlenecks in production.

3. Flow Method

Flow manufacturing is a demand-driven method that is characterized by the continuous flow of units through the production line. This technique is commonly used in the production of televisions and household appliances where the product is manufactured by a number of collective operations in which materials move from one stage to another without time lags or interruptions.

The benefits of the flow method of production are that manufacturers can minimize the number of work-in-process and finished goods items they hold in inventory, reduce costs, and reduce manufacturing lead times.

4. Mass Production Method

Mass Production is very similar to Flow Production. This technique is highly beneficial when producing a large number of the same items in a short period of time.

This type of production is usually automated, which reduces the costs of labour required for production. Some manufacturing facilities have assembly lines dedicated to a specific type of item which reduces the changeover time required and increases the overall production output. This allows manufacturers to increase their profits as the cost of production is greatly reduced.

With this method, operations are scheduled based on the available resource capacity and the production time required at each operation.

5. Process Manufacturing Method

Process Production is a type of continuous process similar to Mass Production and Flow Production but is characterized by the continuous flow of materials through the production line. Usually, the finished goods produced in this type of production are not counted as discrete units. For example, the production and processing of liquids, gases, or chemicals where the product is being produced in a uniform and standardized sequence.

The Process Method uses specific and sophisticated machinery to process materials at each operation step. There is little room for error in this type of manufacturing as changing from one item type to another will require a long changeover period. It is also common to have by-products or waste that result from this type of manufacturing.

Functions of Production Management

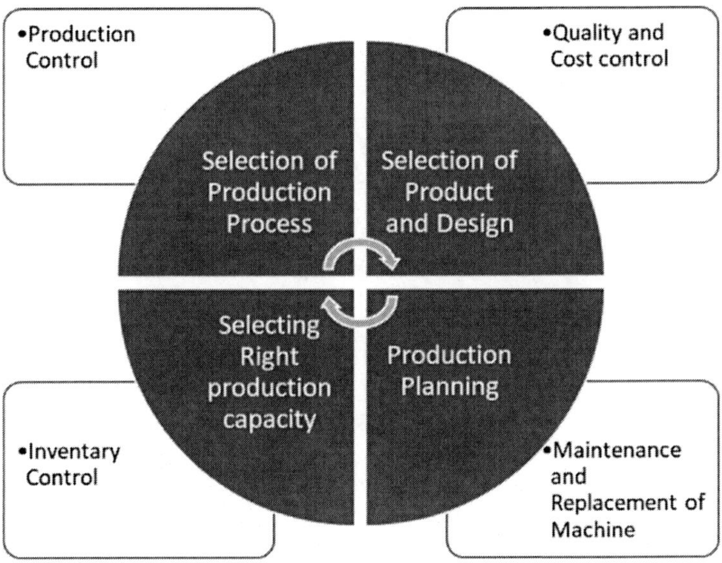

1. Selection of Product and Design

Production management first selects the right product for production. Then it selects the right design for the product. Care must be taken while selecting the product and design because the survival and success of the company depend on it. The product must be selected only after detailed evaluation of all the other alternative products. After selecting the right product, the right design must be selected. The design must be according to the customers' requirements. It must give the customers maximum value at the lowest cost. So, production management must use techniques such as value engineering and value analysis.

2. Selection of Production Process

Production management must select the right production process. They must decide about the type of technology, machines, material handling system, etc.

3. Selecting Right Production Capacity

Production management must select the right production capacity to match the demand for the product. This is because more or less capacity will create problems. The production manager must plan the capacity for both short and long term's production. He must use break-even analysis for capacity planning.

4. Production Planning

Production management includes production planning. Here, the production manager decides about the routing and scheduling. Routing means deciding the path of work and the sequence of operations. The main objective of routing is to find out the best and most economical sequence of operations to be followed in the manufacturing process. Routing ensures a smooth flow of work. Scheduling means to decide when to start and when to complete a particular production activity.

5. Production Control

Production management also includes production control. The manager has to monitor and control the production. He has to find out whether the actual production is done as per plans or not. He has to compare actual production with the plans and finds out the deviations. He then takes necessary steps to correct these deviations.

6. Quality and Cost Control

Production management also includes quality and cost control. Quality and Cost Control are given a lot of importance in today's competitive world. Customers all over the world want good-quality products at cheapest prices. To satisfy this demand of consumers, the production manager must continuously improve the quality of his products. Along with this, he must also take essential steps to reduce the cost of his products.

7. Inventory Control

Production management also includes inventory control. The production manager must monitor the level of inventories. There must be neither over stocking nor under stocking of inventories. If there is an overstocking, then the working capital will be blocked, and the materials may be spoiled, wasted or misused. If there is an understocking, then production will not take place as per schedule, and deliveries will be affected.

8. Maintenance and Replacement of Machines

Production management ensures proper maintenance and replacement of machines and equipment. The production manager must have an efficient system for continuous inspection (routine checks), cleaning, oiling, maintenance and replacement of machines, equipment, spare parts, etc. This prevents the breakdown of machines and avoids production halts.

Four Types of Production

1. Unit or Job type of production

This type of production is most commonly observed when you produce one single unit of a product. A typical example of the same will be tailored outfits which are made just for you or a cake which is made just like you want it.

Example of Unit type of production

It is one of the most common types of products used because it is generally used by small businesses like restaurants, individual products providers or individual services providers.

Types of Production-1

It is also a type of production used by very premium companies like Harley Davidson, or Dell. Harley Davidson actually has a lot of accessories which can be customized, and which suit the individual. Same ways, you can design your own DELL laptop on their website with the given specifications.

Features of Unit production or Job Production

- Depends a lot on skill
- Dependency is more on manual work than mechanical work
- Customer service and customer management plays and important role

2. Batch type of Production

It is one of the types of production most commonly used in consumer durables, FMCG or other such industries where there are large variety of products with variable demands. Batch production takes place in batches. The manufacturer already knows the number of units he needs to a manufacturer and they are manufactured in one batch.

So, if a manufacturer has the shortage of Product X and 100 units of this product is consumed in one month, then the manufacturer can give orders for batch production of 100 units of Product X.

Types of Production - 2

Example of Batch Production

LG has many different types of home appliance products in its portfolio. It has to manufacture all these different variants of the same type of product. There would be 10-20 types of mixer grinders alone in the product portfolio of LG home appliances. Thus, a company like LG manufactures these variants via Batch production.

First, one type of mixer will be manufactured completely and then the second type will be manufactured. They are manufactured on the basis of demand. Depending on demand, the batch production can produce the number of units required in one batch.

The batches may be as small as 10 units or they may be as large as 1 lakh units of the same products. However, as long as there is a defined quantity of product which has to be manufactured before moving on to the next item in the list, it is known as batch production. Examples of batch production include FMCG like Biscuits, confectionaries, packaged food items etc. It is used in Medicines, Hardware, Consumer durables and many such industries.

Features of Batch Production

- Production is done in batches
- The total number of units required is decided before the batch production starts
- Once a batch production starts, stopping it midway may cost a huge amount to the company.
- Demand plays a major role in a batch production. Example - seasonality of products.

3. Mass Production or Flow production

One of the best examples of mass production is the manufacturing process adopted by Ford. Mass production is also known as flow production or assembly line production. It is one of the most common types of products used in the automobile industry and is also used in industries where continuous production is required.

An Assembly line or mass production plant typically focus on specialization. There are multiple workstations installed and the assembly line goes through all the workstations turn by turn. The work is done in a specialized manner and each workstation is responsible for one single type of work. As a result, these workstations are very efficient and production due to which the whole assembly line becomes productive and efficient.

Types of Production - 3

Products which are manufactured using mass production are very standardized products. High sophistication is used in the manufacturing of these products. If 1000 products are manufactured using mass production, each one of them should be exactly the same. There should be no deviation in the product manufactured.

Features of Mass Production

- Mass production is generally used to dole out huge volumes of the product
- It is used only if the product is standardized
- Demand does not play a major role in a mass production. However, production capacity determines the success of mass production.
- Mass production requires a huge initial investment and the working capital demand is huge too.

4. Continuous production or Process production

There is a lot of confusion between mass production and continuous production. It can be differentiated by a single

element. The amount of mechanical work involved. In Mass production, both machines and humans work in tandem. However, in continuous production, most of the work is done by machines rather than humans. In continuous production, the production is continuous, 24 × 7 hours, all days in a year.

A good example of Continuous production is brewing. In brewing, the production goes on 24 hours a day and 365 days a year. This is because brewing takes a lot of time and production is important. As a result, there is a continuous input of raw materials such as malt or water, and there is continuous output in the form of beer or other alcoholic drinks. The key factor in this is that the brewing and fermentation process itself is time-consuming, and the maximum time is spent on the fermentation which is a continuous process.

Types of Production

There are many chemicals that are manufactured in the form of a continuous process due to the huge demand across the world. Similarly, the Plastic industry is known to adopt the continuous production methodology where production can go continuously for weeks or months depending on the demand. Once the production starts, you only need to feed in the raw material, and the machines turn out the finalized products.

Features of Continuous production

- Majority of the work is done by machines rather than humans
- Work is continuous in nature. Once production starts, it cannot be stopped otherwise it will cause huge loss.
- A very controlled environment is required for continuous production.

The "five M's" of Production Management

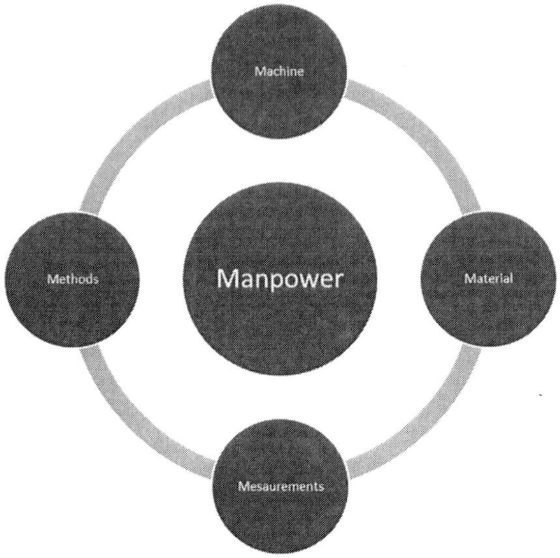

5 M's are:

1. Manpower

It is the responsibility of managers to engage employees in continuous improvement. They must constantly seek feedback and create opportunities for thoughtful changes to process standards. As Taiichi Ohno, the father of the Toyota Production System, said, "Standards should not be forced down from above but rather set by the production workers themselves."

It is also essential that managers recognize and reward those who are contributing to positive change. In fact, improvement should be a key component of employee goals and performance management.

2. Machines (Equipment, Technology)

The need for managers to understand the operation of each piece of equipment and tool in a manufacturing plant is obvious, but technology plays an important role in other sectors as well. In a hospital, for example, "machines" might include medical

equipment and electronic health records and other software applications. Whether it's a physical machine or a software application, managers must ensure that it works as expected and that use of the technology is achieving the desired goal.

3. Materials

In an effort to eliminate excess inventory, a just-in-time model is adopted to chart how materials should flow in a process. Only necessary materials are in the work area. This applies to information work as well as a factory line. For example, new code should not be passed along to a QA department that does not have the current capacity to test it. In healthcare, rarely needed supplies should not be stocked in patient care areas.

4. Methods

"Without standards, there can be no improvement."

Once the best practice for a process is developed and implemented, managers can coach employees on doing their work correctly. Standard work documentation should be made available in the place where work is done and include any useful charts, images, or other assets.

Of course, the standard, while rigorously followed, is not set in stone. Managers lead employees though an improvement cycle whenever an opportunity for improvement is uncovered. A new standard is developed and maintained until the next opportunity comes along.

5. Measurements

In order to know if a process is running smoothly, managers need a set of performance indicators to measure. Not only will they help identify process breakdowns, but they also form the baseline from which improvement can be measured. The most effective measurement tools are visual. People can instantly see when there is an interruption in flow, a definition from typical results, or a task that has not been completed on schedule.

Strategies Used in Production Planning and Control

The main strategies used in production planning and control are the chase strategy, level production, make-to-stock, and assemble to order. A more detailed explanation of these is listed below:

- Chase Strategy (Production Matches Demand) - The chase strategy pertains to the process of chasing demand that is set by the market. Production is set to match demand and does not carry any leftover products. This is categorized as a lean production strategy, simply because it saves costs until the demand, or order, is placed. Within this strategy, inventory cost is low and the cost of goods for products sold is kept to a minimum and in a much timelier manner.
- Level Production (Constant Production Over Time) - Level production is a strategy that produces the same number of units equally. This is very common for industries where demand is cyclical and production capabilities are limited.
- Make to Stock (Enough Product to Stock Shelves) - While make-to-stock may increase inventory cost, it is still beneficial to those that specialize in certain areas, such as retail, cars, phones, etc. Products are made and put in inventory so potential consumers can view what is available.
- Assemble to Order (For Perishables) - This strategy pertains to restaurants or other industries that have perishables to consider. For example, a florist may have to make 50 arrangements but will not make an arrangement until the order is placed. This will reduce spoilage and allows for customization and freshness of perishable products.

A software that can aid with these production planning and control strategies include Planet Together advanced planning and scheduling software (APS). Advanced planning and scheduling software (APS) provide thorough insight into your manufacturing operation through enabling you to generate various schedules

and then ultimately allowing you to pick the most advantageous one. PlanetTogether's APS software has become a necessity for manufacturers around the globe that are seeking to increase efficiency, reduce waste, reduce unwanted costs, and ultimately take production to the next level. APS software has greatly benefited manufacturers across the globe.

Advanced Planning and Scheduling Software

Advanced Planning and Scheduling (APS) software has become a must for modern-day manufacturing operations due to customer demand for increased product mix and fast delivery combined with downward cost pressures. APS can be quickly integrated with a ERP/MRP software to fill gaps where these system lack planning and scheduling flexibility and accuracy. Advanced Planning and Scheduling (APS) helps planners save time while providing greater agility in updating ever-changing priorities, production schedules, and inventory plans.

- Create optimized schedules balancing production efficiency and delivery performance
- Maximize output on bottleneck resources to increase revenue
- Synchronize supply with demand to reduce inventories
- Provide company-wide visibility to capacity
- Enable scenario data-driven decision making

Implementation of Advanced Planning and Scheduling (APS) software will take your manufacturing operations to the next level of production efficiency, taking advantage of the operational data you already have in your ERP.

Strategic management process

The five stages of the process are: setting goals or objectives, analysis, strategy formation, strategy implementation, and strategy monitoring.

The 5 stages of the strategic management process

The strategic management process is more than a set of rules to follow. It is a philosophical approach to business. Top management must think strategically first, then apply that thinking to a process. The process is best implemented when everyone in the business understands the strategy.

1. Goal setting

How to set business goals and strategies. The purpose of setting goals is to clarify the business vision. This stage consists of identifying three facets: First, define the short- and long-term objectives. Second, identify the process of how to achieve the objectives.

Finally, personalize the process according to our staff, give each member a task with which they can be successful. During this process, check that the objectives are detailed, realistic, and coincide with the values of your business vision. Typically, the final step at this stage is to make these goals and objectives known to all staff.

2. Analysis

The analysis is a key stage because the information obtained in this stage will configure the following two stages. At this stage, collect relevant information and data to achieve your vision. The focus of strategic analysis should be to understand the business needs as a sustainable entity, with strategic and identify initiatives that will help the business to grow.

Examine any external or internal problems that may affect your goals and objectives. Be sure to identify the strengths and weaknesses of your organization, as well as the threats and opportunities that may arise along the way.

3. Strategy formulation

The first step in forming a strategy is to review the information obtained from the analysis. Determine what resources the business

currently has that can help achieve defined goals and objectives. Identify any area from which external resources should be sought.

The problems facing the company must be prioritized for its importance to be successful. Once prioritized, begin formulating the strategy.

4. Strategy implementation

The successful implementation of the strategy is essential for the success of the company.

If the overall strategy does not work with the current business structure, a new structure must be installed at the beginning of this stage.

Everyone within the organization must be clear about their responsibilities and duties, and how this fit in with the overall goal. In addition, all resources or funds for the company must be guaranteed at this time. Once financing is in place and employees are ready, execute the plan.

5. Evaluation and control

Any successful evaluation of the strategy begins with the definition of the parameters to be measured. These parameters should reflect the goals established in Stage 1. Determine your progress by measuring actual results versus the plan.

Monitoring internal and external problems will also allow you to react to any substantial change in your business environment. If you determine that the strategy is not moving the company toward its goal, take corrective action. If those actions are not successful, repeat the strategic management process.

Because internal and external issues are constantly evolving, all data obtained at this stage should be kept to help with any future strategy.

CHAPTER 7

Project Management

Project management is the application of processes, methods, skills, knowledge and experience to achieve specific project objectives according to the project acceptance criteria within agreed parameters. Project management has final deliverables that are constrained to a finite timescale and budget. reject management is the process of leading the work of a team to achieve all project goals within the given constraints. This information is usually described in project documentation, created at the beginning of the development process. The primary constraints are scope, time, and budget. It the process of steering a project from the start through its lifecycle. The main objective of project management is to complete a project within the established goals of time, budget, and quality. Projects have life cycles since they aren't intended to last forever.

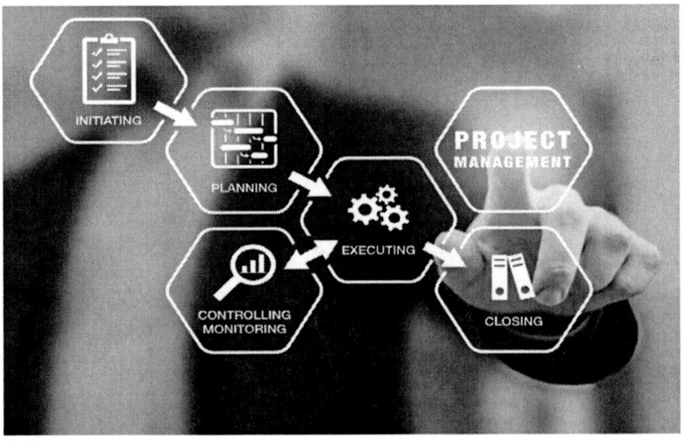

The 5 Project Management Principles of Planning

Principle 1: Create clear and concise project goals

Every project needs goals that are clear, concise, and most importantly, measurable. Without these goals, a project becomes an aimless endeavour that'll never reach any worthwhile conclusion.

The best way to create project goals is to use the S.M.A.R.T. criteria, which stands for:

Specific: Make sure your goal has a specific endgame.

Measurable: Quantify your goals using KPIs (key performance indicators).

Assignable: Make sure this goal is assigned to a specific individual or individuals.

Realistic: Create attainable goals that are achievable in a reasonable timeframe.

Time-related: Set a specific timeframe for your team members to achieve this goal.

This is one of my favourite project management concepts. If your goals don't meet every aspect of the S.M.A.R.T. criteria, they are likely not fleshed out enough to ensure successful delivery.

Setting clear goals serves the dual benefit of tracking progress and also increasing team morale by calling out team member achievements. This morale boost provides motivation for working harder in the future.

Principle 2: Manage your risks

All projects face risks no matter how simple or complicated they might be. The unexpected always happens at some point or another, so it's important to create fail-safes, schedule buffers, and even team backups to ensure you are managing and anticipating risks.

This can be accomplished through team brainstorms, risk assessments, checklists, and response planning.

There are even different types of risk management software options on the market that can help you increase the resiliency of your projects and your company.

If your goals meet all aspects of the S.M.A.R.T. criteria, you are already ahead of the curve when it comes to managing your project's risks since your goals are realistic and tied to a reasonable project time schedule. Always rely on the S.M.A.R.T. criteria.

Principle 3: Establish a performance baseline

There are three basic components of a project plan:

- Cost
- Schedule
- Scope

When planning out these three components, it's crucial to set baselines, also known as KPIs (key performance indicators), to measure them against.

These three components all affect one another, so if your scope must change, so will your costs and your schedule in order to make room for that adjustment. Having a baseline will help you keep these three components in check during the execution phase of your project, even when you need to make changes to your plan.

Principle 4: Establish and maintain healthy communication

Communication is one of the most crucial necessities for project success. Not only should your team feel comfortable communicating with each other as well as you, but you must also maintain a healthy line of communication with your project stakeholders as well.

Encouraging open and consistent communication will help you avoid issues, anticipate risks, resolve project conflicts, and coordinate tasks and schedules in a timely manner.

The project manager is responsible for using your weekly or bi-weekly team meetings to encourage communication between your team members. Use clear examples of issues that could've been avoided had they simply communicated their needs or concerns amongst each other as well as with you.

Principle 5: Clearly define team responsibilities

When you define and outline the responsibilities of your team members, you are actively engaging in risk management that will avoid confusion later on during the execution phase of the project.

RACI charts are an effective means for organizing your team and tracking tasks, milestones, or project decisions.

RACI stands for:

Responsible: Who is responsible for the task?

Accountable: Who will delegate and review the task before it's complete?

Consulted: Who will help review and consult about how current tasks will affect future ones?

Informed: Who will you keep in the loop about overall project progress?

Using a RACI chart will help you set clear expectations so no one is left in the dark about who needs to do what, where, and when. Build your RACI charts around primary project tasks that affect the deliverables rather than administrative to-dos such as meetings or developing project reports.

Phases of the Project Management

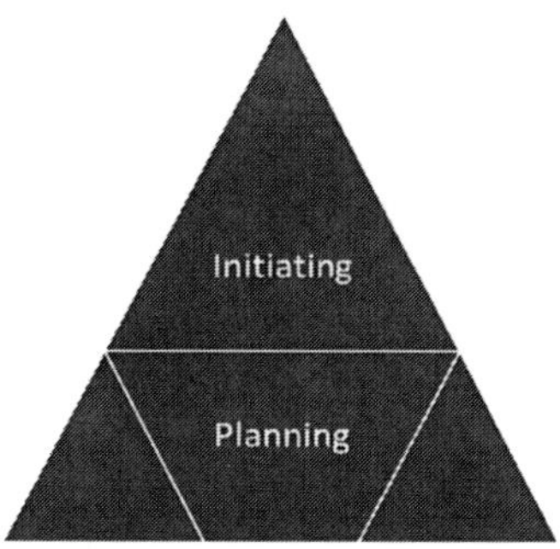

1. Initiating

In the initiation phase, you'll define the project. You'll sort out the project goals, scope, and resources of the project, and what roles are needed on the team. Clarifying what stakeholders expect out of the project, and what exactly the project is aiming to achieve (and why) will give the project and team clear direction.

This is a crucial phase to the project's success. Without clarity around what needs to be achieved and why, the project runs the risk of not accomplishing the end goals and meeting the expectations of stakeholders.

Some steps in the initiation phase include:

- Communicating with stakeholders to understand the purpose and desired outcomes of the project
- Identifying project scope
- Determining SMART goals (specific, measurable, achievable, relevant, and time-bound)
- Clarifying resources like budget and time constraints
- Confirming team size and roles required
- Determining how often and which stakeholders will be involved throughout the project
- Compiling a project proposal and project charter

Tools and documents used in the initiation phase can include:

- Project proposal: The project proposal defines a project and outlines key dates, requirements, and goals.
- Project charter: This is a definitive document that describes the project and main details necessary to reach its goals. This can include potential risks, benefits, constraints, and key stakeholders.
- RACI chart: A RACI chart plots the roles and responsibilities of members on a project team.

2. Planning

In the planning phase, you'll determine the steps to actually achieve the project goals–the "how" of completing a project.

You'll establish budgets, timelines, and milestones, and source materials and necessary documents. This step also involves calculating and predicting risk, putting change processes into place, and outlining communication protocols. If the initiation phase is assembling your troops,the planning phase is deciding what to do with them.

The planning phase can include the following steps:

1. Deciding on milestones that lead up to goal completion
2. Developing a schedule for tasks and milestones, including time estimates and potential time buffers
3. Establishing change processes
4. Determining how and how often to communicate with team members and stakeholders
5. Creating and signing documents such as non-disclosure agreements (NDAs) or requests for proposal (RFPs)
6. Assessing and managing risk by creating a risk register
7. Holding a kick-off meeting to start project

Tools you might use in this phase include:

- Gantt chart: A horizontal bar chart in which members can see what tasks must be completed in what order, and how long each is expected to take
- Risk register: A chart that lists risks associated with the project, along with their probability, potential impact, risk level, and mitigation plans.

3. Execute and complete tasks

Executing a project means putting your plan into action and keeping the team on track. Generally, this means tracking and

measuring progress, managing quality, mitigating risk, managing the budget, and using data to inform your decisions.

Specific steps might include:

1. Using tools like GANTT or burndown charts to track progress on tasks
2. Responding to risks when they manifest
3. Recording costs
4. Keeping team members motivated and on task
5. Keeping stakeholders informed of progress
6. Incorporating changes via change requests

Some tools you might use include:

- Change requests: These are documents used to propose changes to a project's scope or goals
- Burndown chart: This chart breaks down tasks on a granular level and visualizes the amount of time remaining

4. Close projects

In the closing phase of the project management lifecycle, you'll conclude project activities, turn the finished product or service over to its new owners, and assess the things that went well and didn't go so well. It'll also be a time to celebrate your hard work.

Steps in the closing phase can include:

1. Conducting retrospectives and take notes of changes you can implement in the future
2. Communicating to stakeholders of the end of the project and providing an impact report
3. Communicating with the new owners of a project
4. Creating a project closeout report
5. Celebrating the end of the project and your successes

Tools used in the closing phase include:

- Impact report: This report compiles a series of metrics that showcase how your project made a difference and is presented to your stakeholders.
- Project closeout report: A project closeout report provides a summary of your project's accomplishments, and provides key learnings for future project managers to reference.

4 Types of Projects in Project Management

A person who is going nowhere can be sure of reaching his destination.

For example, if you are unsure of what is to be done and unsure of how to go about doing it, you are likely to feel as if you are caught in the fog.

Your gut feeling may be one of fear, loss, confusion, or uncertainty.

Obeng describes four types of projects:

- Walking in the fog
- Making a movie
- Going on a quest
- Painting by numbers

Understanding the four types of projects can help you to predict problems and put measures in place to avoid them. And the leadership styles needed to deliver organisational change are closely related to each type of project.

1. Walking in the Fog

If you don't know what you want or how to achieve it you are likely to have a "walking in the fog" type of project.

Typically, the organisation is attempting to do something different. Something that hasn't been attempted before. These types of projects are started because of a change in circumstances.

For instance, introducing a new business strategy in response to political, legislative, or socio-economic organisational change. As such, this type of change project calls for certain leadership styles: tight control, strong communication, and innovation and creativity.

These projects require teamwork and a desire to work and learn together.

Walking in the fog projects should proceed cautiously. If not, you risk delivering nothing of benefit to the organisation.

2. Making a Movie

If you know how but not what you need to do you, have a "making a movie" type of project.

In this situation, your stakeholders are very certain about how the project should proceed but not what needs to be done.

Your organisation has built up significant expertise and capability in the area the project will tackle and has many people committed to the methods needed to deliver the change.

During the early stages of this type of project you need to focus your attention on solving the what—writing a business case—not the how.

That is, mobilise problem solvers from within your organisation or use external sources to develop and generate ideas. Once you have your script, the movie will make itself.

"Vision is the art of seeing things invisible." - Jonathan Swift

Making a movie type of project evokes positive emotions and a sense of purpose and openness.

3. Going on a Quest

In contrast, the "going on a quest" type of project is where you and most of your stakeholders are very sure of what should be done. However, you are unsure how you will achieve it.

Long-range purposes keep you from being frustrated by short-term failures.

If you are involved in this type of project you will no doubt feel challenged, excited, or single-minded. Projects involving information technology tend to fall into this category and are often criticised for cost overruns, being late, or not delivering the expected benefits.

Consequently, your leadership style needs to balance strict control of time and cost with the freedom to innovate and solve problems.

Above all you need a team of self-motivated people— "knights" —who work tirelessly to seek out and then deliver the solution.

4. Painting by Numbers

The "painting by numbers" type of project is where you always want to be by the time you start investing lots of time and money in the change project.

You and most of your stakeholders are sure of what to do and how it is to be done. These change projects tend to have clear goals plus a clearly defined set of activities needed to complete the project.

Areas within Project Management

The Project Management Institute (PMI) has identified nine areas of knowledge within project management:

1. Integration management

Integration management is the coordination of all elements of a project. This includes coordinating tasks, resources, stakeholders, and any other project elements, in addition to managing conflicts between different aspects of a project, making trade-offs between competing requests, and evaluating resources.

The 7 steps of project integration management

Project integration management offers a holistic approach to project planning and execution. The practice consists of seven processes to effectively coordinate project activities. Let's break them down.

The 7 steps of project integration management

A. Create project charter

Projects typically start out with the creation of a project charter, a short document that provides an overview of the project and identifies the project manager and key stakeholders.

- A project charter includes the following:
- Scope
- Objectives and deliverables
- Project team members
- Project risks
- Benefits or returns on investment
- Budget
- Business case

A project charter essentially acts as a foundation on which you can further plan your project. It also helps you gain buy-in from stakeholders, which enables you to move forward quickly and autonomously within the project scope.

B. Develop project management plan

The next step involves developing a more detailed project plan, which specifies the project scope statement, deliverables, timeline, milestones, and metrics to evaluate success.

The project plan is used to direct the execution of the project to meet overall requirements and objectives.

Here are the steps to creating a project management methodology:

1. Meet with stakeholders to set project requirements, deliverables, and objectives.
2. Define the project scope.
3. Create a work breakdown structure (WBS) to delegate tasks and assign resources.
4. Create a project schedule.

5. Conduct a risk assessment and develop contingency plans.
6. Come up with a performance measurement baseline to assess project performance.
7. Develop additional plans for any of the following: scope management, cost management, resource management, change management, stakeholder management, or risk management.
8. To help you with this process, you can use a project planning template as a starting point to build your plan.

9.Free cross-functional project template

C. Direct and manage project work

The next phase is project execution, in which the project manager takes charge of the day-to-day work that must be done, such as:

- Directing the project team
- Holding stakeholder meetings
- Tracking project progress
- This phase ensures that tasks are being carried out effectively according to the project plan and scope statement.

D. Manage project knowledge

Project knowledge management refers to the process of using existing information or obtaining additional knowledge to reach project goals. This step ensures team members have all the information they need to produce the required deliverables.

Any knowledge or expertise gained during this step contributes to the company's overall body of knowledge, which is useful for future strategic endeavours.

E. Monitor and control project work

Since processes in project integration management are interconnected, they should be followed closely to ensure that everything adheres to the project management plan.

The purpose of this step is to keep the project on track. If there are any deviations from the project plan, they need to be identified and corrected.

There are three approaches to this:

- Preventive action: an action performed to reduce the negative impact of project risks
- Corrective action: an action performed to bring the future project performance back in line with the project plan
- Defect repair: an action to repair or replace a documented project defect

A common technique to measure performance is to do an earned-value analysis to assess the current status of the project's budget and schedule. If project changes need to be made and are approved, project documents such as the work performance report may need to be updated.

Monitoring the project ensures that it is on track to meet objectives.

F. Perform integrated change control

Changes to projects can sometimes be stressful if not handled properly, but with a change control process in place they don't have to be.

That's why change requests must be assessed to ensure they don't exceed the scope or approach scope creep, which refers to the increase in requirements during the project lifecycle. Some companies even have a dedicated change control board to review change requests related to budget, timelines, and resources, for example.

An example of project change is if the client asks for additional assets, in which case you'll need to evaluate the level of impact on the project.

Use a change control log to document all change requests, including which ones were approved, the associated costs and resources, and how they impact the project timeline. Smooth integration of change requests to current project activities is crucial for the success of the overall project.

G. Close out the project

After all project work is complete and deliverables are shipped and approved by the client, it's time to close the project.

Project closure involves processes such as:

- Holding a final stakeholder meeting
- Conducting a formal review of the project
- Closing the contract
- Organizing and archiving project materials for future use

Project closure serves as a reference for future endeavours and provides insight on how to improve the project integration management system.

2. Scope management

Scope management is a process that helps in determining and documenting the list of all the project goals, tasks, deliverables, deadlines, and budgets as a part of the planning process. In project management, it is common for a big project to have modifications along the way.

With the scope of the project management defined right in the beginning, it becomes much easier for project teams to manage and make the required changes.

Scope management process

A. Planning scope management

In the first process in project scope management, you create a scope plan document that you can refer to in the later stages. The

document mainly helps in defining, managing, validating, and controlling the project's scope.

It includes:

- Detailed project scope statement
- Breakdown of all the project requirements
- Expected project deliverables
- Project change control process

The document doesn't have to be very detailed; it just has to fit the purpose. You can also use a previous project's scope management plan as a reference for this.

B. Collecting requirements

The next step is to work out stakeholder requirements and expectations. You will be required to document all the project requirements, expectations, budgets, and deliverables through interviews, surveys, and focus groups. This is a rather important step because more often than not, stakeholders can have unrealistic requirements or expectations and the project managers would be required to step in to find a solution that is acceptable by everyone from avoiding project delays.

At the end of the collection requirements stage, you should have the following:

- Functional as well as non-functional requirements
- Stakeholder requirements
- Business requirements
- Support and training requirements
- Project requirements

C. Defining the scope

At this step, you need to turn your requirements into a well-detailed description of the service or product that you are trying

to deliver through the project. You will then have a project scope statement that you can then refer to throughout your project.

While it is important to list what is in the scope of the project, it is just as important to note down what is out of the project scope. Any kind of inclusions to the scope would then have to go through the entire change control process to ensure the team is only working on things that they are supposed to work on. With a defined scope, you get a reference point for your project team and anyone else involved. In case there is something that is not involved in the scope, it doesn't need to be completed by the team.

D. Making a project breakdown structure

A project breakdown structure is a document that breaks down all the work which needs to be done in the project and then assigns all the tasks to the team members. It lists the deliverables that need to be completed and their respective deadlines as well.

You can use project management software for this step of the process to assign and prioritize project tasks which will make it easier to track the entire progress of the project and avoid any unnecessary bottlenecks.

E. Validating scope

In this step, the scope and deliverables that you have recorded need to be sent to project executives and stakeholders to get the necessary approvals. Scope validation needs to be done before starting the project to ensure that if something goes wrong then it is easy to find where it went wrong.

F. Controlling scope

Project managers need to ensure that as the project begins, it always stays within the defined scope. In case there are some things that need to change, then the proper change control process should be followed.

3. Time management

Time management helps you prioritize your tasks so that you ensure you have enough time available to complete every project.

The quality of your work increases when you're not rushing to complete it ahead of a fast-approaching deadline.

The 4 Ds of Time Management

Productivity starts with a well-organized schedule. The 4 Ds of time management strategy helps product managers schedule, postpone, or discard tasks by placing them in four categories: delete, delegate, defer, and do.

- "Delete" encourages product managers to learn to say "no" and carefully filter their to-do list. Product managers should delete clutter work – such as junk mails and non-vital meetings – to make room for core matters.
- "Delegate" should include tasks that don't require the specific know-how of a product manager. Reassigning work is one of the most efficient strategies of time management, as long as the new person-in-charge has the required skills to fulfil the requirement.
- "Defer" can be used by product managers to postpone tasks that are not-time sensitive. Whether it's a new request or a project with an extended deadline, work that can be postponed in favour of immediate priorities should be.
- "Do" is as straightforward as it gets. Product managers need to start working on these tasks immediately and focus their attention on one at a time until they get them done.

4. Cost Management

Cost management is a method of reducing operating or production expenses in order to provide less expensive products or services to consumers. In other words, it's the process management uses to analyse its production and streamline its operations to keep costs low and manage expenses in the future.

Process of Cost Management

1. Resource planning

While resource management is in place to plan, allocate, and schedule the resources needed for each stage of a project, resource planning looks specifically at the costs associated with each of these resources. Because of the complexity of this process, a work breakdown structure (WBS) can help to simplify and provide clarity. Using your resource planning software, identify what resources will be used to complete each item in the WBS, determine the associated costs, and perform a cost-benefit analysis.

2. Cost estimation

Cost estimation is the process of approximating the costs associated with each of the resources required for all scheduled activities. Cost estimating forecasts the cost of completing a project within a defined scope. Given that scope tends to shift throughout the life of a project, cost estimation is not a one-time process. Effective cost management requires project managers to iterate on cost estimations whenever scope changes or change requests are approved. These estimations provide a summation of all costs involved in successfully finishing a project, from inception to completion.

To get a good estimate at the costs, you can use one of the following techniques:

Analogous estimating: estimates are based on past projects. It uses actual costs from a similar finished project to estimate the costs of the new project. The accuracy of these estimates will depend on the similarities between the new project and the old project.

Parametric modelling: estimates are based on mathematical formulas, typically following a Regression Analysis or Learning Curve model. The accuracy of these estimates depends on the assumptions made.

Bottom-up estimating: estimates are based on individual work item cost and duration estimates. This involves estimating the

smallest activities and then adding them up to create an estimate for the whole project.

3. Cost budget

Cost estimations lead directly into the cost budgets. In this step, you will determine the cost baseline and the funding requirements for the project. A good project budget will help you make key decisions with respect to the project schedule and resource allocation constraints. Combine individual activity cost estimates into a total project cost, establish the timing of the costs, and measure the progress of the project against the approximated baseline costs. These budgets should account for everything from direct labor costs, to material costs, factory costs, equipment costs, administrative costs, and software costs.

To determine the cost budget, consider the following techniques:

- Cost aggregation: requires you to aggregate or combine costs from an activity level to a work package level. The final sum of the cost estimates is applied to the cost baseline.

- Reserve analysis: requires you to create a buffer or reserve to protect against cost overruns. The degree of protection should be equivalent to the risk foreseen in the project. The buffer is part of the project budget, but not included in the project baseline.

- Historical data: requires you to think about estimates from closed projects to determine the budget of the new project. This is very similar to analogous estimation described earlier.

- Funding limit reconciliation: requires you to adhere to the constraints imposed by the funding limit. The funding limit is based on the limited amount of cash dedicated to your project. To avoid large variations in the expenditure of project funds, you may need to revise the project schedule or the use of project resources.

4. Cost control

Good project managers will carefully monitor the cost of their projects to prevent scope creep. This includes watching to see where actual cost has varied from estimated cost. Cost control also involves informing the stakeholders of cost discrepancies that vary too much from the budgeted cost.

Controlling the budget requires being aware of the original budget, approved costs, forecasted costs, actual costs, and committed costs. If there are any changes to scope or if unforeseen risks have an impact on the approved budgets, the project manager will need to review the level of impact and take corrective action as needed.

To effectively control project costs, consider these tools and techniques:

- Earned value management: uses a set of formulas to help measure the progress of a project against the plan.
- Forecasting: uses the current financial situation to project future costs. The forecast is based on budgeted cost, total estimated cost, cost commitments, cost to date, and any over or under budgeted costs.
- To-complete performance index (TCPI): represents the level of project performance that future work needs to be implemented to meet the budget.
- Variance analysis: involves analysing the difference or variance between the budgeted costs and the actual costs to indicate whether the project is on budget.
- Performance reviews: used to check the health of a project. Includes an analysis of project costs, schedule, scope, quality, and team morale. By learning how to estimate costs, determine budgets, and control costs, you can be a better project manager and leader. Effective cost management will help you get projects done on time and under budget, the golden ticket for any successful project manager.

5. Quality Management

Quality management includes everything we do to make sure we produce and deliver our company's products and services to spec and at the appropriate cost. Quality management also includes making sure goods arrive on time. It ensures that a company's goods or services are consistent.

Quality management focuses both on product and service quality and on the means to achieve it. It has four main components: quality planning, quality control, quality assurance, and quality improvement.

STAGES OF QUALITY MANAGEMENT

Quality Through the Project Lifecycle

The four main components of a quality management process are Quality Planning, Quality Assurance, Quality Control and Continuous Improvement.

Quality Planning

Determines which quality standards are necessary and provides guidance to stakeholders on how quality management will be performed on the project. It will include:

- Stakeholder expectations - this section should document specifically what the customer expects in terms of project quality. Including whether they have specified any external quality standards and what their priorities are in terms of the areas affected by quality.
- Success criteria (as defined in the business case) in addition to the defined success criteria this section should also define acceptable tolerances for achievement of those objectives.
- Standards applicable (internal and external) - the project environment may require that the Quality Plan incorporates the requirements of external standards. These

could range from the Company's own quality standards to ISO 9000 or Health and Safety at Work Legislation.

- Roles and responsibilities concerned with quality - these may include quality assurance testing, supervision and management roles
- The process that will be followed - these will be documented in a systematic way and will govern the mechanisms for the product of the product specifications and testing procedures.
- How continuous improvement will be actioned - this may include making adjustments to processes where they are proven to be unsatisfactory.
- Project assurance techniques - This section will describe how assurance will be performed and who is responsible. It will define policies of quality reviews and audits of the management process.
- Quality control measures - will define control measures that will be used
- Interactions with other processes such as configuration management, change control and how these links will be established.

Quality Assurance

Quality reviews are a key tool for quality assurance but could also be used for quality control. The way they will be conducted will be set out in the Quality Plan. Four overall objectives for review:

- Provide assurance that the project is proceeding according to agreed plans/processes.
- Measure effectiveness of agreed plans/processes
- Capture lessons learned
- Identify areas of non-compliance and opportunities for improvement

Quality Assurance covers the whole project lifecycle and is not concentrated on any particular phase. It ensures that the other processes (mainly Planning and Control) are being adequately performed and that the project is adhering to any corporate standards that are relevant to the project.

Quality Assurance involves pre-planned, regular reviews and independent audits to verify that work is being carried out consistently in accordance with defined procedures and to provide confidence to stakeholders the project will satisfy relevant quality requirements and standards.

Quality Control

Quality control consists of inspection, testing and quality measurement verifies that the projects deliverables conform to specification, is fit for purpose and meet stakeholder's expectations. Quality control techniques are varied and the technique used should be driven by the nature of the project. The most obvious example of quality control is the inspections and tests that are done to check whether a product meets is specification. The exact inspection method used depends entirely on the technical nature of the product being developed by the project. Inspections that may be relevant:

- Construction - part of Quality Control would be to check the strength of the concrete.
- Aircraft - part of Quality Control would be to check the quality of the welding.
- Process - part of Quality Control may be to pilot before making live. Having inspected the products and gained the data on their performance, we need to identify any problems and understand the causes - tools that can be used to display the inspection data are:
- Histogram - Plots frequency of variables. The height of the bar shows how often a particular result occurs and the number of bars indicates the range of results

- Scatter Chart - used where there are 2 variable and we want to see if there is a relationship between them, i.e. the strength of number of cubes against recorded outside temperatures may show relationship between strength and temperature.
- Control Chart - plots value for each of a number of outputs of the same process. It also sets tolerances for the values measured. This allows us to identify if the process is in or out of control. For example, plotting the results for the test of each weld on the ship to ensure our welding process was within acceptable control limits
- Run Chart - plots the history of a single variable. For example, if a key performance criterion for a project was the variance between actual and cost, this variable could be plotted over time to track its variation and identify trends. Tools for understanding causes or prioritising areas for action:
- Pareto Chart - this is a type of histogram that orders the information in a particular way. This is sometimes called the 80:20 rule; 80% of the observable faults are caused by 20% of the root causes. This enables us to direct problem solving where it will be most effective.
- Process Control Chart - A graphical representation of a process showing activities and decision points. A flow is used to show how different parts of a system interrelate. It can help the project team identify where quality problems may occur or redesign a process to correct problems.
- Cause and Effect - is simply a graphical technique to help develop an understanding of how certain causes may lead to a particular effect. This section may also define how the project should control change and perform configuration management

Continuous Improvement

There may be opportunities to improve management processes during the life of the project or information that

assists the management of future projects. Continual systematic approaches to quality improvements such as adherence to Total Quality Management (TQM), Six Sigma or any external industry standards, can be used.

This is part of corporate governance - if there is a variance on a project then it must be corrected, however the root cause of the problem must be understood to ensure that the same problem does not occur on further projects. A continuous systematic approach to Quality Management creates steady growth and improvement to keep a company focused on its goals and priorities.

6. Communication Management

Communications management is an umbrella term referring to the flow of information within a company or between multiple companies. It focuses on reaching a company's target audiences–consumers, employees, vendors, media groups, etc.–by planning and implementing myriad methods of communication. Both internal and external communications management play an essential role in the overall health and vitality of any business.

Communications management process

There are 3 primary steps in the communications management process:

1. Plan communications
2. Manage communications
3. Control communications

Plan communications

You can start managing your project's communication strategy by creating a communications management plan. The communications management plan needs to document communications requirements throughout the life of a project. Some of these requirements include:

Cadence: How frequently are updates going to be sent out?

Audience: Who will project communications be sent out to? Is there a different group for different types of communications?

Purpose: Will progress reports be sent out at each milestone? Will change requests be shared with all stakeholders?

Channel: What channels will be used for communication?

The communications management plan should include as much detail as possible so that there are clear expectations set and all stakeholders are on the same page.

Manage communications

Now that all stakeholders have agreed on the communications management plan, the project manager needs to ensure that project communications follow those guidelines. The communications plan should be seen as a living document throughout the life cycle of a project, but any changes should be communicated to the project team.

Control communications

Not all stakeholders find relevance in every project detail. Because of this, only include stakeholders on communications when necessary. Create sub-groups of stakeholders to decide what types of communications they need to receive. These include project status, project performance, risks, costs, and others. Being effective in controlling communication streamlines project management and saves project leaders and team members from getting irrelevant updates and emails.

7. Risk Management

Risk management is the process of identifying, assessing and controlling threats to an organization's capital and earnings. These risks stem from a variety of sources including financial uncertainties, legal liabilities, technology issues, strategic management errors, accidents and natural disasters.

Types of Risks:

Risk can be referred to like the chances of having an unexpected or negative outcome. Any action or activity that leads to loss of any type can be termed as risk. There are different types of risks that a firm might face and needs to overcome. Widely, risks can be classified into three types: Business Risk, Non-Business Risk, and Financial Risk.

- Business Risk: These types of risks are taken by business enterprises themselves in order to maximize shareholder value and profits. As for example, Companies undertake high-cost risks in marketing to launch a new product in order to gain higher sales.
- Non- Business Risk: These types of risks are not under the control of firms. Risks that arise out of political and economic imbalances can be termed as non-business risk.
- Financial Risk: Financial Risk as the term suggests is the risk that involves financial loss to firms. Financial risk generally arises due to instability and losses in the financial market caused by movements in stock prices, currencies, interest rates and more.

8. Procurement Management

Procurement management is responsible for overseeing all the processes involved in acquiring the products, materials, goods and services needed for efficient business operations.

4 main processes of project procurement management

Project management for procurement is usually divided into four major processes: planning, selection, administering and closing procurements.

1. Planning

The first part, planning, involves the creation of the official procurement management plan. The decisions made involve which items will be internally procured and which items will be externally

outsourced. This information, in turn, will heavily impact the project's budget and financial scope. Sample procurement documents will be prepared, and criteria frameworks will be developed to create a selection of potential vendors. This selection matrix is based on the project's scope, schedule, and requirements. Risk factors and budgetary constraints are also considered.

2. The Selection Process

The selection process involves comparing and contrasting vendors' advantages, disadvantages, and contractual offerings. Standard tools and techniques are used to select procurements, such as video conferences with bidders that allow them to understand the project requirements and ask questions. Procurement contracts are decided and awarded through collaborations between various managers. Resource calendars are then created that detail when, where and how resources will be used and managed. The corresponding project management plan is adjusted according to resource calendar updates. Proposals are carefully evaluated and if no satisfactory bids are available, the project management team may utilize online ads to solicit new bidders.

3. The Administration Process

The third major step is administration, which refers to the tools and processes used to manage relationships with vendors. The administration phase results in the continual creation of procurement documents and spreadsheets that may drive project changes. A centralized system of contract change monitoring and control will be used to evaluate and determine whether potential changes to contracts are needed. There are formal physical inspections, internal audits and reviews of procurement operations in order to generate synthesized performance reports that provide real-time feedback. The administration process is extremely important, so it's usually managed through supply chain or project management software.

4. The Closing Process

The closing process is not just about ending procurement contracts; it's about noting weaknesses, documenting successful processes and summarizing the project for future needs. Some companies prefer to conduct simple audits using performance matrices to grade the overall project. Documentation is important for future projects, which may involve entirely different teams in new locations. During the closing process, negotiations may be necessary to resolve contract disputes. Ideally, potential issues will be noted during the administration process to begin the mediation process early. When it comes to project procurement management, there are standard features and functions. For example, most companies prefer to use a smaller number of suppliers with long-term relationships instead of using a group of suppliers to outbid each other for the lowest price. Establishing and nurturing relationships with suppliers is important because this enables various supply chain partners and shareholders to work closely together on improvement and coordination activities.

CHAPTER 8

Knowledge Management

Knowledge management (KM) is the interdisciplinary process of creating, using, sharing, and maintaining an organization's information and knowledge. It is a multi-faceted strategy for making the best use of organizational knowledge assets in order to achieve business objectives such as enhancing competitive advantage, improving performance, boosting innovation, sharing insights, and continuously improving the organization. Knowledge management systems are therefore part of the organizational learning process, although they focus more on strategic management of knowledge as a shareable business asset. The core goal of knowledge management is to connect people looking for knowledge within an organization to those who have it, with the ultimate aim of increasing the overall knowledge level of the team and organization. Four knowledge management objectives assist in reaching that goal. Those goals are: improving the knowledge capture process, streamlining and enhancing the knowledge environment, increasing access to organizational knowledge, and maintaining knowledge as an organizational asset.

Components of Knowledge Management

People

You've probably heard the phrase, "people, process, and technology." Since at least the early 1990s, organizational leaders have used this paradigm–often referred to as also the "golden triangle"–to guide initiatives and lead organizational change. The idea is, if you over-focus on one factor, your initiative is bound to fail. And the order is important: you need to get the right people involved before you get into processes and technology. When you're starting a KM program, you need two kinds of people:

Senior leaders to provide sponsorship and insight into broader organizational strategy, and cross-functional stakeholders to guide implementation.

Senior sponsors should be visible, engaged business leaders who have something big to gain from the implementation of KM. Often, they're people who lead business areas with major, urgent knowledge needs (e.g., experts are retiring, new hires can't get up to speed quickly). In selecting cross-functional stakeholders, look first to your colleagues in HR, IT, and process improvement–APQC research shows collaborating with these functions improves effectiveness.

As thc KM effort matures, most organizations staff up a KM core team, identify KM champions and facilitators across the business, and establish an executive steering committee to provide ongoing stewardship. If you think this sounds like a lot of people, you're right! You need engaged people at different levels and in different areas of the business to really build knowledge sharing into the culture. But that doesn't mean you have to spend a ton of money or take away too much time from folks–especially if your processes are smart, your content and IT infrastructure isn't cumbersome, and your strategy is compelling.

Process

In organizations with strong KM processes, knowledge flows like a city water supply: when someone needs it, they just turn the tap. The KM team, like a city planner, knows how everything flows beneath the surface. They can identify bottlenecks, reroute flows, and measure inputs and outputs. But the end user doesn't need to understand how all that stuff works. For them, getting the knowledge they need is simple and easy.

APQC has identified a standard knowledge flow process that describes how knowledge flows through organizations. It's a seven-step cycle:

1. Create new knowledge (this happens every day, all the time, across all areas of the business)
2. Identify knowledge that is critical to strategy and operations
3. Collect knowledge so it can be shared with others
4. Review knowledge to evaluate its relevancy, accuracy, and applicability
5. Share knowledge through documentation, informal posts, and collaborative activities
6. Access knowledge through pull (e.g., search) and push (e.g., alerts) mechanisms
7. Use knowledge to solve problems faster and make more informed decisions.

For KM teams, the key is to identify ways to build these steps into the business processes people already use every day. For example, you can build knowledge collection into stage gates, or integrate knowledge review into certain job roles. Technology tools can also help with this–by, for example, delivering relevant alerts in the flow of work–but ultimately, you need to understand people's processes first.

AF528438

વિકાસનો પથ

સંસાર પ્રસિદ્ધ વિચારક અને
લેખક શ્રી સ્વેટ માર્ડેનનાં
પુસ્તકોએ કરોડો લોકોના
જીવનમાં ક્રાંતિ લાવી
દીધી છે, ભટકી રહેલી
માનવતાને નવી દિશા આપી છે.

પ્રસ્તુત પુસ્તક
'વિકાસનો પથ'
પણ આ જ મહાન વિચારકની
મહાન કૃતિનું ગુજરાતી રૂપાંતર છે.